MY FAVORITE CASHEW

C.B. ANDERSON

WestBow
PRESS
A DIVISION OF THOMAS NELSON

Scripture taken from the King James Version of the Bible.

Scripture taken from the New King James Version. Copyright 1979, 1980, 1982 by Thomas Nelson, inc. Used by permission. All rights reserved.

WestBow Press books may be ordered through booksellers or by contacting:

WestBow Press
A Division of Thomas Nelson
1663 Liberty Drive
Bloomington, IN 47403
www.westbowpress.com
1-(866) 928-1240

ISBN: 978-1-4497-5794-6 (sc)
ISBN: 978-1-4497-5795-3 (hc)
ISBN: 978-1-4497-5793-9 (e)

Library of Congress Control Number: 2012911701

Printed in the United States of America

WestBow Press rev. date: 07/16/2012

To

My Children
Daniel and Martha
Ben and Amanda
Sam and Laura
Lily

My Children's Children
Emerson
Baby Anderson

The Patients and Friends of
Carroll County, Indiana, and Beyond

All the Wounded Children That Cry Alone in the Night

Thomas R. Anderson, M.D.

Contents

Foreword

I WAS MEETING DR. TOM ANDERSON for lunch one day. It was our time to get together outside of church. While I was waiting for him at his office, he invited me back to his exam room.

"Sit down there, and put those things over your eyes," he said. "I'm going to laser that dark spot off your forehead."

When he was done, I asked, "Do I pay the girls at the desk, or will they bill me?"

"Nah, forget it. Let's go to lunch" was his reply.

That was Dr. Tom Anderson. He saw a need and filled it. Money was not his goal in life. Serving his Lord and Savior, meeting the needs of people and patients, and caring for his family were the things that what mattered to him.

I was privileged to know Doc, as he was called at our church, only for three years before God called him home. He is greatly missed to this day. He was a tremendous man, a tremendous man of God.

His wife has captured his life in this book as no one else could have. No one knew better what he went through than the loving helpmate God gave him. They walked through joys and struggles together.

There are two important aspects in this book. One of them is what a man goes through in life after suffering from child abuse and the added burden of manic-depressive disorder. The other is the importance of the love, compassion, and understanding necessary to support a person with these issues. With love and support, there can be hope, good times, and a very productive life.

I highly encourage anyone struggling with these same issues in their life or in the life of a family member, to find the love written between the lines in this book. These issues that beset Doc were terrible things. Nonetheless, he chose to keep going. In doing so, he became unique and special to many people. If you need encouragement and understanding, you will find it in these pages.

Our dear friend left us early in life on Thanksgiving morning. Hundreds of people miss him and continue to mourn his death. Why so soon, we may wonder. I believe God was pleased with his life and felt he had suffered enough.

Doc was quite a character. He always had a witty comeback. I can't wait to hear how he responded when God said, "Well done, thou good and faithful servant: thou hast been faithful over a few things; I will make thee ruler over many things. Enter thou into the joy of thy Lord."

Ken Smith, Pastor
Hickory Grove Church
Delphi, Indiana

ACKNOWLEDGEMENTS

THANKS TO GLORIA HEBER, MY prayer partner, for helping me edit and encouraging me.

Thanks to my daughter, Martha, for helping me edit and cheering me on.

Thanks to my son, Ben Anderson, for his medical and psychological perspective.

Thanks to my son, Sam Anderson-Been, for his electronic formatting.

Thanks to my daughter, Lily, for sharing her journal entry.

Thanks to Westbow Press for making it happen.

CHAPTER 1

THE MAN IN THE GARDEN

As he stood up in the middle of the church flower bed, brushing the dirt from his hands, the sun cast golden highlights on his light-brown hair. His neatly trimmed beard had auburn accents. Behind his round, wire-rimmed glasses, his blue eyes squinted in a shy smile. His black-and-red plaid jacket made him look like a broad-shouldered woodsman, even though he was on Lunt Street in Chicago.

That was one of the first times I noticed Tom Anderson. Years later, on our twenty-fifth wedding anniversary, I would give him a card that said, "If I had to choose all over again, I would still choose you!" And, I would. In spite of the demons that haunted him, I would choose Tom Anderson all over again.

It was early spring of 1977, when a Christian sister whispered in my ear to "check out" a brother named Tom Anderson. Ever so slowly, Tom and I began to take notice of each other at church activities and at school. He was a pre-med student at Northwestern University, where I worked in the accounts payable department. At the beginning of the semester, he came hesitantly to my window to pay his tuition. We chatted lightly. When our church decided to start a lunchtime Bible study on campus, we both attended.

Always a little late, Tom would come bobbing into the classroom with his distinctive walk. Whether it was the turn of his hip or a slightly shorter left leg, we were never sure, but he was easily recognized in a moving crowd with his slight bounce from side to side as he hurried from one place to another. His button-down, oxford shirts, creased pants, and round, wire-rimmed glasses conveyed an old-fashioned aura that contrasted sharply with the faded blue jeans, pony-tails, and tie-dyed T-shirts of the late seventies.

One afternoon, at the end of our lunch-time Bible study, Tom leaned over and asked, "Do you like to ice-skate?"

Having waited for weeks to get better acquainted with him, I quickly responded, "Sure. I'm not great at it. I mean, I've only skated on corn-fields that flood in the winter and freeze over. So, I'm good at dodging things like cornstalks protruding through ice, but I don't do anything fancy."

"That's okay. I'm just learning. I'll meet you by the pond at 6:30 p.m. on Friday." Then, he was out the classroom door and down the hall.

After two or three Friday evenings of ice-skating, he shyly took my hand and pulled me forward as he skated backward. Skating led to ice cream dates, snow skiing at Mt. Trashmore (a waste disposal site turned into a ski slope) in Evanston, Illinois, and finally, trips to his family homestead in Illinois, and mine in Indiana. Tom's family retained ownership of a 550 acre farm in Illinois, which had been passed down from his grandparents to his parents. His family did not personally farm the property, but Tom liked to visit the rural homestead.

We also enjoyed visiting where my family lived in rural, Carroll County, Indiana. My Dad and Mom baled hay, raised hogs, and harvested crops on their land.

Leaving Chicago and going to see my family in Indiana, meant a weekend of castrating young male hogs, baling hay, or any other farm work that needed to be done. The least favorite of these jobs, castrating hogs, meant hours of tackling fat, male pigs who needed to have their testicles cut off. No farmer wants to raise a herd of virile male hogs, which would barrel through fences to breed with the females. Neither does a farmer want to be docked at the sale barn for trying to sell fat hogs with their reproductive glands still attached. The best prices are paid for neutered livestock. However, farmers are notorious for not getting those male organs off soon enough. Hence, the job often involved wrestling a too-big hog, holding him down, slicing with a surgical knife, and pulling out testicles the size of baseballs. The squealing alone reverberated in the eardrums for hours after the job was done. Tom never shirked any of the farm work, but rolled up his sleeves and cut, yanked out, and flipped over his shoulder as many hog testes as anyone.

One weekend, the most pressing job was to clean out the oat bin. My brother, who was a law-school student at that time, Tom, and my dad, shoveled dusty oats for several hours one Saturday afternoon. That night, all three of them started shaking with chills, coughing, and spitting up black mucus. They each had been affected by the mold spores in the oat dust. Tom would vividly remember this illness when he treated many farmers during his medical practice in rural Indiana.

A weekend of visiting Tom's family farm in southern Illinois, did not involve nearly as much hard labor. We stayed with his brother and sister-in-law who moved near the farm after they finished college. We drank his brother's homemade wine, talked until the early hours of the morning, and cooked out at the cabin his brother had built on a wooded hillside at the farm. Tom showed me the farm pond and told me about the famous, local, burgoo cook-off in the near-by town. Regardless of which farm we escaped to from the city, Tom's passionate love for the land and preference for a rural lifestyle were evident.

When we returned to Chicago, Tom would adapt himself just as diligently to academics as he did to farm labor. With the intent of applying to medical school, Tom worked very hard to earn top grades. But, for him, medical school was about more than acquiring knowledge and skills. On his application to medical school, he wrote:

> Shortly before high-school graduation, I had a deep Christian experience that caused me to completely re-evaluate all of my ideals. At that time, I was planning a career in medicine, but I had to interrupt those plans because I felt the need to work full-time in a Christian ministry. I spent the next eight months talking to people about my Christian experience. During this time, I traveled throughout the United States, talking to all kinds of people with every kind of need. I learned a lot about people. I found that I was able to help some people with their problems; but, for most people, I could do little. I found out that people needed more than just my words; they needed my help in a practical way, a way which would speak stronger than my words. I felt that the most practical way for me to help people would be by becoming a physician. My next nine months were spent working in a greenhouse and a chemical factory in order to earn money for school.
>
> During my first four quarters of school, I reconsidered my goals many times. Medicine seemed to be the perfect way for me to help people, yet I had one fear-that the pressures of the educational system, coupled with the opportunity to make a considerable sum of

money, might change me into a person who would be more materialistically-oriented rather than people-oriented. It was uppermost in my heart that I would not allow this to happen. For this reason, I changed my major to another interest: horticulture. In order to change majors, I had to change schools; therefore, my transfer was made to Triton College. Within three weeks after my transfer, I realized that horticulture was not the profession in which I belonged. I loved people, and I loved medicine. I became determined to do two things: to apply myself to the utmost in school in order to make a way scholastically for me to get into medical school; and, to not allow anyone or anything to make me be materialistically-oriented rather than people-oriented. I felt that a more competitive school would increase my opportunity for acceptance into medical school, so I transferred to Northwestern University and have pushed toward this goal ever since.

During this time, I have done volunteer work at Evanston Hospital, along with work as an orderly in their operating room. Currently, I am working in pancreatic cancer research at their laboratories. These experiences, plus two more years of maturity, have made me fully aware that medicine is where I belong.

Along with his grades and personal statement, Tom needed an academic referral for his application to medical school. His chemistry professor at Northwestern University, Dr. Carroll King, gladly wrote his recommendation:

"Anderson is a remarkable young man. By conversation, I have learned he was not too sure of himself in the beginning, but when he discovered he could compete favorably with college students, he made his move to medicine. He has had work experience as a gardener, and I think a cabinetmaker. He displays none of the hysteria so common in today's pre-med students. He just goes to work quietly and does the job. He never seems to be distracted. Please note–I have read your instructions, and I do not believe my estimations are inflated. In my opinion, Anderson is the best pre-medical student I have ever encountered."

As Tom was excelling academically, our dating relationship was coming to a standstill. Although we enjoyed each other's company and loved visiting our family homes, neither of us seemed to be sure we were right for one another. We talked it over and decided to stop dating. Tom had previously been engaged to a young Christian woman in our church who had returned his ring and called off the engagement. She felt unable to wait for him to finish college before getting married. She was ready to meet someone and start a family; he wasn't. Tom decided to see if she was still interested in him, while I decided to return to my college studies in literature, after having worked for a couple of years to earn money.

Our separation was short-lived. The young woman Tom had known was seriously dating someone else and had no interest in returning to her old relationship. I enrolled at Northern Illinois University in DeKalb, Illinois, and sent Tom a card with the following message: "So, I'm sorry things didn't turn out. Did you ever think maybe we had something worth working on? You know, we could just be friends. If you ever want to go for ice cream or coffee, just let me know."

Tom immediately called and asked me to go with him to the Lutz Pastry Café in Chicago. We stood in line, talking as if we had never been apart. As we made our way back to the car, Tom said he needed to tell me something that he hadn't shared with me before.

We sat in the car, licking our icing-covered fingers while our breath fogged the windshield. Streetlights stood like shrouded sentinels peering through the mist, listening quietly to our conversation.

"I should have told you when we first met."

"Told me what?" I raised my eyebrows, dreading what he might say because of the tone of his voice.

Remember me telling you that I moved from the farm when I was four to live in Clinton, Iowa?"

"Yes, I remember."

"Well, growing up in Clinton was hard for me. I was the youngest of my siblings, and I was very lonely. My folks were pretty busy, but there was this friend of the family, an older man ..."

In the stilted silence, I knew what he was going to say. My heart ached for him.

"He molested me." Although Tom was staring straight ahead, I could see a tear slide down his check.

My heart sent urgent, muted prayers to heaven for wisdom and words beyond my own. Sliding my hand in his, I said softly, "That wasn't your fault or your choice, you know. And, that isn't who you are. I see a man beside me who is full of integrity, kindness, and compassion, with a brilliant mind and a noble ambition to serve Christ through serving people. Besides, don't you think we all come to Christ with a whole bundle of stuff from our past? Let's just go on from here. But, thank you for telling me."

We said no more about his past. The past would have its own voice in the years to come, but we didn't know that at the time. We just knew we were happy to be together again. We decided that although neither of us was very good at dating, we had missed each other terribly. Even though Tom was busy with graduation preparations that spring, we spent as much time together as possible.

We saw the first *Star Wars* movie, held hands as we walked through the Chicago Botanic Garden, and clutched the rollercoaster handlebars at the Great America amusement park. By the spring of 1978, we knew we wanted to spend the rest of our lives together; but, the future looked complicated. Tom was accepted at the University of Iowa Medical School, and I was enrolled at Northern Illinois University. Our schools were four hours apart. We decided to get married in June. However, it didn't work out that way.

"I can't marry you," Tom half mumbled while looking away and holding my hand.

We sat on the white rocks of the north shore of Lake Michigan. I let my eyes follow the sailboats gliding across the lake in the crisp currents of a spring breeze. The gentle wind blew long strands of my dark-brown hair against my cheek.

Brushing back my hair, I asked, "Do you love me?"

"Of course I love you!" His voice choked with frustration, "It's my parents. They don't think I will finish medical school if I get married now."

"You remember that I have my dress picked out and the church reserved, right?"

"I know. But, I can't convince my parents." The agony in his tone contrasted sharply with the tranquil, sun-kissed beach.

"They don't like me, do they?"

"I don't know." He shoved his hands deep in his pockets. "My mother tells everyone that you are petite, willowy thin, and very intelligent; but, she told me that I should just have you live with me instead of marrying you. She knows I won't do that!"

I stared for a long time at the water lapping against the rocks at my feet before saying with a smile, "Well, I'm not really willowy or petite. I'm five feet, four inches tall, and that is pretty average. You might call me slender, but, definitely not willowy. Anyway, look, we can deal with this. You go ahead and go to Iowa. I'll go to school at DeKalb. We'll just see what God does, okay? If you and I are meant to be together, we'll figure it out."

I slipped my hand in his as we walked along the bike trail by the lake. He squeezed my hand and said softly, "We can call each other, and I'll come and see you. You can come and see me, too."

We each started our classes in the fall of 1978. Every evening, after eleven, when telephone calls were free, the phone would ring in my apartment. After about six weeks of these calls, Tom became insistent. "I can't do this. I'm too lonely," he pleaded. "Please marry me. I want you to be here. Besides, I made friends with a Mormon guy in my class, and he has a wife and a beautiful baby girl. I want one of those little girls!"

"I can't get married until next spring when school is out," I said. "But, I'll come and see you. Do you think your parents will agree to our marriage?"

"It doesn't matter. It was crazy for me to come out here without you. I need you with me. It's way too hard to be here alone. Let's get married between the semesters. Please, say yes!" I said yes. Because I was busy with classes and lived four hours from home, my amazing mother planned the details of our wedding. Weekly checklists came through the mail with fill-in-the-blank phrases:

I want the icing on my cake to be_____.

The bridesmaid dresses will be_____.

The ushers will be_____.

Special music will be provided by_____.

Flowers on the reception tables will be_____.

I filled in the blanks and returned the pages as quickly as possible. In the meantime, Tom had received word from his parents in New York, where his father had been transferred, that they were unable to attend the wedding. We stood on the steps outside my apartment at DeKalb.

"Why can't they come, Tom?" I tried to keep the disappointment and hurt from showing in my voice.

His shoulders slumped. "Mom said they can't afford the trip."

"It doesn't make sense! Your dad has a degree in chemical engineering and a very good job. Your mother is a college graduate with a science degree, and they own a 550-acre farm. Most people their age were fortunate to finish high school. There must be enough money for plane tickets, or at least money for gas to make the drive."

"Look," he said with sad resignation, "there is a place on the Iowa campus that offers payment if you sell them your blood for the plasma. I am going to sell my blood. I'll be able to save enough to send them the finances for plane tickets."

"No, Tom, you can't do that. You'll get tired and sick, and you won't be able to keep up with your studies. If they can't make it, we can cancel the wedding. You can't get married without your parents." He leaned down and kissed my lips. "We are getting married in December, and one of these days, we are going to have one of those beautiful baby girls."

We married on December 30, 1978, between semesters of college. Shortly before the wedding, Tom received word that his parents would be attending and that they didn't need his "blood money." In an attempt to improve our relations, we drove to upstate New York and spent time with his parents on our honeymoon before returning to classes in Iowa City. I enrolled as a transfer student at the University of Iowa, and Tom continued his classes at the medical school.

For years, Tom kept a file of mementos in his cabinet. One of the sayings he liked was: "I didn't say it would be easy; I said it would be worth it. - Jesus." There were many things we faced together through the years that were not easy, but, yes, it was worth it.

CHAPTER 2

THE CHICKEN LADY AND JESUS

M Y MEMORIES OF FARM LIFE included a lot of hard work, so I was curious about what sparked the yearning in Tom to return to a rural lifestyle. Knowing that he was not entirely comfortable talking about his early childhood, I would gently prod information from him about his memories of the farm and his move with his family to Clinton, Iowa.

"I loved Bill," he told me one afternoon. We were nestled into our one-bedroom apartment that was a few blocks from the medical school. I sat cross-legged on the couch while he reclined in his favorite chair. We were trying to study, but ended up talking instead.

"Bill was our dog. I just remember that every place I went, Bill went with me. My mother said he was my babysitter. I remember him licking my face and sitting beside my stroller in the yard. I was only four years old when we moved from the farm. I hated leaving Bill."

"Why didn't you just take him to Clinton with you?" I asked, being a dog lover myself.

"I was too young. It wasn't my decision, anyway. Besides, in Clinton, I had Adelle."

"Who was Adelle?" I asked, stretching out on the couch and settling in for a good conversation.

"Adelle was sunshine, hugs, and hot cocoa in a five-foot bundle of energy. She helped with the household responsibilities when my mother went to work. She made me treats, and she made me laugh. I think Adelle loved me very much."

I looked down at my book, pretending to study. There were things I didn't understand about Tom's childhood. He had so few memories, and those he did have were so different from my own. I remember my mother acting out nursery rhymes with us after supper, reading *Heidi* to us at night until our eyes got heavy with sleep, tucking us in bed, and playing "The Fairies Wedding" on the piano outside our bedroom door. I remember my father building us a wooden boat, painting it red, and helping us crawl in and float on the creek. We could easily stand up in the water, but we loved to sit in the boat and pretend we were going to a far-away place. I remember riding behind my father on his horse and clinging tightly to his waist, confident that wherever we went, I would be safe. One day in particular that I remember, we had a severe winter storm with a layer of ice on everything, but school wasn't cancelled. The lumbering yellow bus came to a crawling stop in front of our house. My father went out the door and talked to the driver. Dad refused to let us ride the bus that day; it was too dangerous, he said. He kept us home, stayed with us, and hitched the sled to our donkey. That donkey pulled us all over the icy fields until the sun melted through our fun.

It seemed impossible to me that Tom could recall so few family experiences from his past. I wondered if he had misconstrued his childhood, or if there were elements that did not surface in his memory banks because of the molestation.

Laying aside my book, I suggested, "Let's go out. Let's go to The Mill and listen to bluegrass music."

The Mill was a popular bar and restaurant in the late seventies and early eighties. The food was reasonable, but the live music was even better. Being on a student's budget, we ordered drinks and listened to the bluegrass band. I wanted to laugh and to forget the confusing picture of Tom's childhood. For me, there was an unspoken poignancy in the few stories he recalled. It wasn't always the things he said that troubled me; many times, it was the things he didn't say.

Listening to bluegrass music was a great escape from our classroom routine. But our poverty as students provided other opportunities as well for togetherness and a change of pace from our studies. One of the things Tom admired about rural people was their ability to live off the land and be self-sufficient. So, when our food supply ran short, we applied our resourceful, mid-western survival skills to help put meat in our freezer - sometimes to the dismay of our fellow apartment occupants.

We needed meat, and Tom had been given the name of a farm woman who raised and sold chickens about twenty miles from town. Early one Saturday morning, we drove along the dirt roads and the gentle hills outside Iowa City to the home of the "chicken lady."

Her yard was cluttered with broken pieces of machinery, rain-soaked cardboard boxes, rusty fragments of wire fence, and grayish-white piles of chicken poop scattered like a mine-field. Two dogs of an unrecognizable breed circled beneath a tree on tight chains, yapping incessantly.

Tom navigated his way through the yard just ahead of me. I leaned over his shoulder and asked, "You sure you want to buy chickens here?"

"I heard she raises good meat chickens and that the price is reasonable. Don't worry. We'll boil anything we eat," he assured me.

Before we reached the house, a heavy-set, smiling woman, waving a butcher knife in her hand, came bustling out the screenless, wooden porch door.

"Hi, kids," she greeted us warmly, "Ten chickens, right? I'll have them ready in no time. It only takes me a jiffy to get those heads off, and I got a machine for the feathers."

We followed her through the yard as she sloshed along in her size-ten rubber boots and hoisted up her faded, blue-jean shorts that threatened to reveal more than we wanted to see of her posterior. I was pretty sure her sweatshirt was on backward. It was stretched tightly across her back fat with the emblem of a semi-trailer followed by the words: Keep on Truckin'.

Thankfully, we didn't have to chase anything. We arrived at a small cage of ten well-fed, squawking chickens. Without the slightest hesitation, the chicken lady reached in the door, grabbed a bird by the neck, slipped it out, gave one quick twist to its neck, and hacked off its head. She carried it a few feet away to a sagging clothesline and, with a piece of blood-soaked baling twine, tied the dead chicken by its feet so the blood would drain. This procedure was rapidly repeated nine more times while Tom and I watched.

As soon as the job was done, she turned with her now blood-splattered face, and said, "Grab a couple of 'em, kids. We'll haul 'em up by the house and get these feathers off."

Sure enough, one of the machines in the yard actually worked. It was an automatic chicken plucker. In a matter of minutes, the feathers were off, and the naked chickens were soaking in a galvanized-metal tank full of cold water.

Wiping her bloody hands on her shorts, Chicken Lady invited us in for a cup of coffee while the chickens "chilled down." She kicked her boots off just inside the door and padded across the kitchen floor. I stared at the white feathers clinging to her bare feet with sticky, red blood, and I whispered to Tom, "Make sure she boils the coffee. Don't drink anything that hasn't been boiled, okay?"

"You know," Tom said, looking at his watch, "we really have to get back. We don't have too far to drive. It's only about twenty minutes. I have some buckets in the car. I think we'll just load those chickens up and head home. But thanks for the offer."

He handed her the agreed-upon payment, and we took our buckets to the water tank. Lifting out dripping-wet chickens and loading them into our buckets took only a few minutes. Heading back toward town, we laughed about the colorful Chicken Lady we had left behind. It wasn't a mocking laugh; we both appreciated her skill and efficiency in raising nice meat chickens, which they were. But she was quite a character.

We carried the chickens into our apartment in the buckets. Setting them in our tiny kitchen, I said, "We probably should have gutted these at her place. We're going to have the entrails and feet from these chickens to deal with, you know."

"I guess I didn't think of that," Tom said. "Let's get them cleaned out; then, we'll figure out what to do with the guts."

For the rest of the afternoon, we sliced through the skin and pulled out the entrails of the ten chickens, which we dumped back into the buckets along with the feet. We cut up five of the chickens, bagged them, and put them in the freezer. The other five we boiled so we could preserve the meat and broth in canning jars.

As we picked meat off the bones, Tom remembered another time of canning chickens. "When we left the farm and moved to Clinton, I remember canning chickens in the basement of our farm-house. My grandpa had passed away by that time, and Grandma had control of the land and the finances. Dad worked for Grandma on the farm in those years, but I guess she didn't let my folks have any money. Leaving the farm was an escape for my parents. We had to can chickens in the basement so we would have food to live on when we moved to Clinton, where Dad got hired on as an engineer at the corn processing plant."

"Why was your Grandma so mean that your family had to sneak away?" I asked.

"I don't know for sure. I don't think she and my mother ever liked each other. Grandma had a lot of money and a very strong personality. I remember the year she bought a pink purse and then went out and bought a pink Cadillac to match it. I also remember Grandma saying she could shoot the eye out of a chigger with her rifle. She wasn't the kind of woman you messed with. But, you know," he said it almost wistfully, "I think Grandma loved me.

"Wasn't there anything you liked about the move to Clinton, besides escaping from a domineering grandmother?" I asked.

"Not much." He sighed. "I was a very bad child. By the time I was nine, I was smoking a pack of cigarettes a day."

"What! Why did your parents let you do that?"

"Oh, they didn't know," he replied matter-of-factly.

Glancing at Tom's face, I wondered if he really believed that his parents didn't know he was smoking cigarettes. I remembered my uncle, who had tried to quit smoking for twenty years. His clothes, his car, his house, and his breath reeked of cigarette smoke. The lingering odor from consuming a pack a day would be impossible to conceal, especially for a nine-year-old kid.

"Did you like school?" I pried, hoping to find something favorable in his experience.

"Well, I went to Catholic school, you know, so there were a lot of restrictions."

The dress code for boys required button-down shirts, ties, and pants with no outside seams, which would eliminate any possibility of blue jeans showing up on the school grounds. But Tom had a great aunt who lived in Arkansas, and she was an excellent seamstress. She came to visit, and Tom asked her to sew him a pair of pants with no outside seams. The pants met the school requirements, but they were made with a patchwork of multi-colored taffeta in shades of hot pink, neon orange, lime green, and every other color ever created.

"So, how long did you last?" I asked, smiling when he told me the story.

"Not long." He grinned. "They hauled me to the office and out the door so fast I couldn't even argue. But it was worth it."

"At church, I was a lot worse," he continued. "My friend and I were altar boys. Every Sunday, we stood like little cherubs at the front of the church. Then, as soon as we got the collection plates to the back room, we each pocketed about a hundred dollars, and we guzzled the left-over communion wine."

"Wow! Didn't you feel guilty?" I cringed.

"Nah, not at the time. I needed the money for cigarettes and drugs. Most of my high-school years, I roamed the streets on weekends and got high. My brother's friend sold me LSD. It's funny, but even though I was using drugs, I had good grades. I actually competed very well on the debate team, too, in spite of my drug use. If I hadn't become a Christian, I'm pretty sure I would have died from an overdose."

I put the chicken bones down on the kitchen table and scooted my chair close to Tom. Putting my head on his shoulder, I said, "I'm really glad you became a Christian, but I'm sorry you went through such painful, lonely years in your life."

He shrugged. "Maybe I wouldn't have needed Jesus if it hadn't been for those years."

Tom didn't go looking for Jesus; Jesus came to Tom. It was one of the weekends when Tom's parents were out of town. Alone in the house, he took his usual dose of LSD. But this trip was different from the others. It was more vivid. Tom was in a place he had never been before; he had heard about it only in church. He visited hell.

With a distant look in his eyes, Tom remembered the "trip" he made into hell. "The only light was from the fires. They burned everywhere. People were scattered throughout the darkness, but they didn't burn, even when the flames licked them. There was a sorrow and an emptiness that was deeper than any black hole in space. Every soul there was tormented. There was a memory, a consciousness that brought agony to each inhabitant. I could hear the weeping, sometimes screaming. It was a cry of mental and emotional pain filled sometimes with regret - other times, with hate. And, you know what? People really do gnash their teeth in hell. There is no place as hopeless as that dark, sulfurous pit in the deep center of our earth. I was there. The ground was solid beneath my feet, even though the fires were everywhere. I was terrified. Then, there was a light coming near me out of the blackness. It was warm and pleasant. Out of the brightness, Jesus walked. He held out his hands to me. There were scars from the nail holes. He said He was there to rescue me. I reached out my hands to Him."

Tom smiled then. "It's funny, but I didn't become a Christian that day. I woke up in the snow outside our house. I had broken the glass in the door, and my hands and bare feet were covered in blood. My parents were pretty upset with me when they came home."

A few months later Tom committed his life to Christ. An evangelist was holding a revival meeting in a tent on the outskirts of town. There was a raging thunderstorm the night he stood at the back of the tent, rain soaking his shirt, and puddles swirling around his feet as he listened to the speaker. The evangelist asked for people to come forward who wanted to give their heart and life to Christ.

Tom prayed one of the first honest prayers of his life: "God, I really want to commit my life to You, but I am embarrassed to walk in front of all those people. Please help me."

The thunder boomed, and the lightning flashed. The tent lights flickered and then went out completely. In the dark, Tom groped for the aisle and ran forward. When the lights came on, he was standing with several other people who had gathered at the front to make a personal commitment to Jesus Christ. Through God's great mercy and power, he released Tom that night from his addictions to both cigarettes and hard drugs.

As we sat at the table in our little apartment, canning chicken, I told Tom, "Seems to me that God went to a lot of effort to rescue you. He must have something special in mind for your life."

He laughed and said, "Yeah, well, I hope He also has a plan for these chicken guts, because I just remembered that the trash pick-up isn't until Thursday."

"I thought you had this all figured out," I chided.

We stuffed the entrails and feet into garbage bags and shoved them to the bottom of the metal trash barrels on the basement level of our apartment. By Tuesday, we could hear residents gagging from the smell when they opened the doors to the building. Tom and I passed neighbors on the stairs and never said a word. On Thursday, we sighed with relief as the garbage man, full of complaints, hauled out the reeking bags of trash (and chicken guts). We were thankful for cans of chicken on our shelves and meat in our freezer. And I was thankful that one very lonely, troubled young man found a Savior.

CHAPTER 3

LICE AND PIZZA

MOST STUDENTS HAD RELATIVELY LITTLE money in the late seventies and early eighties. Tom and I were no different. But Tom had known poverty and hunger in a way that neither I nor most other students could even imagine.

After Tom became a Christian, he wanted to become involved in full-time ministry. With only the money in his pocket and the clothes he could fit into a knapsack, he joined the Jesus People. During the sixties and seventies, the Jesus People traveled across the country, living in tents that were carried from town to town by a caravan of semi-trailers, preaching the gospel to everyone who would listen.

Tom made two very good friends while traveling with the Jesus People: Tobias and Zoe. Tobias had been a practicing transvestite before becoming a Christian; Zoe had been a practicing witch. After choosing to follow Christ and join the tent ministry, both young people became fast friends with Tom. Together, the three of them passed out Bible tracts, shared the gospel from street corners, sang, and gave testimonies in coffeehouses, and occasionally, feasted at a restaurant.

" practicing transvestite"?

It was late. A frigid November wind plucked at the backs of the three gospel messengers. Huddled together for warmth, they stumbled down the street toward a late-night diner. They pushed the door open and scooted into a warm booth. Tom, Zoe, and Tobias had handed out tracts and led the singing during the presentation of the gospel at the evening's tent meeting. But they were reluctant to return to their frigid sleeping bags on the cold, hard floor of the tents.

"Anybody got any money?" Tobias asked. His shoulders were still hunched from the cold.

Zoe rubbed her hands together and replied, "Yeah, right! You know we have to turn all our money over to the big guys. I don't have two nickels to rub together."

"She's coming over to our table." Tom pointed at the baggy-eyed waitress, whose shoulders slouched with an exhaustion that weighed down her smile as well as her shuffling feet.

"Whaddya kids want?" She exhaled as she asked.

Zoe and Tobias looked at Tom. Zoe shrugged. Tobias opened his mouth to speak, but Tom quickly interjected, "three cups of hot water, please."

"Figures." She sighed as she pivoted away.

As soon as she set the steaming cups of hot water on their table, Tom grabbed the ketchup bottle. Squeezing a sizable helping into the cup of water, he passed the bottle to Tobias; then he stirred his watery gruel.

"Look, guys, this is how you make tomato soup," he said. "Go ahead. It isn't bad."

Tobias and Zoe took turns squeezing the ketchup into their cups. Holding the steaming "soup" in their hands, they sipped slowly, savoring every bit of flavor.

"Well, it beats day-old donuts and oatmeal," Tobias said. "How long do you think it's been since we've had anything besides starch to eat?"

"I don't know," Tom said, "but it seems like we take in an awful lot of money at the meetings. And we have to give the leaders everything that comes from our parents. You would think maybe we could have something decent to eat once in a while."

"You know, guys, I love Jesus, and I love telling people about my Jesus," Zoe said. "He set me free from some wicked people and some evil powers. But I've never been so hungry in my life as these past few months."

Tom was quiet, mesmerized by a starry-eyed couple two booths away, who were holding hands around a steaming pizza loaded with meat and cheese. Slowly, he scooted out of his seat and walked to the couple.

Brushing back his hair from his forehead, he pleaded in his most humble voice, "You know, if you two aren't going to eat that pizza, my friends and I are really hungry. We would love to have it before it gets cold."

For a moment, the infatuated couple looked at him as if he was a recently landed alien, and then they shoved the pizza toward him. He quickly carried it to the table where his friends drooled in anticipation. Sliding the pizza onto the table, he grinned and said, "It's feast night!"

Food was scarce, but warm sleeping bags were also in short supply. In the winter, the tent people moved south where the winters weren't so bitterly cold. Still, sleeping outside on the ground was much colder than a warm bed in a heated house. The traveling young people cherished what little warmth they could generate in their less-than-adequate sleeping bags, especially on the nights when tiny flakes of snow sifted down outside the tents.

On one of those frosty nights, Tom found a drunken man stretched across a sidewalk grate. Bending down, he shook the man by the shoulder. "You've got to get up, sir. Listen, you'll get frostbite. You need to come with me."

The elderly man rolled over and sat up as if in a dream. "I have no place to go," he slurred.

"Yes ... yes you do," Tom told him as he pulled the man to his feet and helped him stand. Pulling the man's arm around his shoulders and reaching his other arm around the man's waist, Tom guided him back to the tent. Once there, he gently laid the man in his sleeping bag, tucked him in, and zipped it up. Tom slept on the ground that night, shivering until the morning sun wrapped its warmth around his cold, stiff shoulders. When he awoke, the man was gone.

Several days later, Tom began to scratch his scalp incessantly. He was crawling with lice. He washed his hair with kerosene and turned his sleeping bag inside out after a good de-lousing. Did he regret sharing his sleeping bag with a man who left no other thank-you than an infestation of lice? "No," Tom always said, "I think that is what Jesus would have done."

Another way Tom and his friends reached out to people was by visiting coffeehouses. During these years, coffee-houses sprang up everywhere. Many of these houses were for songfests, aspiring musical bands, and amateur preaching. Tom sang. He admitted later that he suspected it was the sincerity of his heart rather than the quality of his voice that the people loved. One of the popular coffeehouse songs from those years that Tom frequently sang was "I've Been Redeemed." Singing into the microphone and swaying to the music, he declared with all his heart:

> I've been redeemed, I've been redeemed,
> By the blood of the Lamb, by the blood of the Lamb,
> I've been redeemed by the blood of the Lamb, filled
> with the Holy Ghost I am,
> All my sins are washed away, I've been redeemed.

There were many verses to this song. Some of the other verses were:

> You can't get to heaven in dirty blue jeans, 'cuz heaven
> ain't got no washing machines.

You can't get to heaven on roller skates; you'd roll right by those pearly gates.
You can't get to heaven in powder and paint, 'cuz God won't take you how you ain't.
You can't to get heaven by smoking pot; you'd think you're there when you're really not.

Most people loved the kindness and sincerity of the young gospel preachers associated with the tent ministry, but not everyone. The only time Tom ever went to jail was during his year with the Jesus People. On a street corner across from a public high school in Austin, Texas, Tom and his friends collided with local police. As the tent people handed out tracts to students, police cars and a paddy wagon pulled onto the scene. The Jesus People were loaded into the paddy wagon and delivered to the city jail. The official Austin police report reads as follows:

> At about 7:46am, November 1, 1972, while on patrol, this officer received a call to Reagan High School in regard to subjects loitering on the school ground. Upon arrival at the above location, this officer observed thirteen subjects walking on the sidewalk in front of the school, passing out religious leaflets to the students and singing religious songs.
>
> Shortly thereafter, this officer was approached by John P. G. McKenzie, the head principal of Reagan High School, who told this officer that he had warned the religious individuals to leave the school grounds and to stop handing out leaflets, in which they failed to abide by his warning, and [he] then called [the] police. Mr. McKenzie stated that J.R. Viramontes, the assistant principal, would file on the subjects for loitering on school grounds.

Under question number thirty-five of the police report, which asks, "Exactly what did offender say?" This response was recorded: "Amen, brother. Jesus saves, and God bless you brother."

Tom was fingerprinted and booked that night along with the other "offenders." They spent a memorable night in jail and were released the next morning.

As the semi-trailers loaded equipment, young people, and work crews for their next stop in San Antonio, Tom was thinking a lot about his future. During his year of traveling the country with the Jesus People, he had met a lot of people, including other Christians.

One of the Christian men he encountered had told him, "Tom, God loves people who are willing to leave everything behind them to go out and preach the gospel, but sometimes people need more than words. Believe me. God needs people who have skills, talents, and daily responsibilities as well as those who aren't tied down by such commitments. If you are feeling like you should go back to school, you had better do it."

Tom knew he wanted to go to college. He said a sad good-bye to Tobias, Zoe, and his other friends from the past year. Walking several miles through a light snow, he found a pay phone and called a relative who lived just outside San Antonio. For the first time in a year, he slept in a real bed and ate a balanced meal. His parents wired him the money to fly home to Clinton.

He went home only to gather his belongings and catch a bus to Chicago. His heart and mind yearned to be able to help people in a practical way. There were good schools in Chicago, and he had already been given the name and phone number of members from a strong Christian community. He would find them, and, without anticipating it, he would also find his future wife and soul mate.

CHAPTER 4

FROM THE WINDY CITY TO *AMERICAN GOTHIC*

THE YEARS TOM LIVED IN Chicago were devoted to outreach and street ministry, as well as rigorous pre-med college studies. The church he belonged to in Chicago - with more than 250 members of all ages, professions, and ethnicities - was a close-knit group with a family atmosphere. Unlike churches in many established denominations, it was led by six ministering elders and six deacons instead of a single pastor receiving a salary. One of these elders was employed as a public-school teacher and offered to rent a room in his home to Tom. The elder's wife, also a teacher, treated Tom like a son. In this church community, Tom offered his gardening skills to help maintain the flowerbeds in front of the church building.

Tom and I both rode the trains, ate ethnic food, enthusiastically participated in inner-city outreach, and took advantage of opportunities available only in the "big city." But we longed for a more rural setting. Moving to Iowa City after our wedding enabled us to move just a little closer to the lifestyle we longed for. Although the city itself was very progressive, it was surrounded by Amish and Mennonite communities as well as thousands of acres of farm ground.

Reading the paper one Saturday morning, Tom noticed an ad for red raspberries. "Look at this! Some Amish farm is selling all-you-can-pick raspberries. Let's go get some."

"How do you know that it's an Amish farm?" I asked, reluctant to leave my summer-school books or to forfeit my lazy Saturday.

"Well, the Amish don't have telephones, so they just put an address in the paper. There's no phone number in this ad, but I know I can find this place. Let's go before everybody gets there and picks all the berries ahead of us," he insisted, pocketing his keys and walking toward the door as he spoke.

"Okay," I said with marginal enthusiasm. Tossing aside Chaucer's *Canterbury Tales*, I slipped on my shoes. As I skipped down the apartment stairs and out into the July sunshine beside Tom, it felt good to be going on a trip to the countryside, even if it did mean work when we got there. We hopped in the car and left the city behind us. Tom easily located the farm, not more than thirty minutes from town. We could see the rows of berries as we pulled up to a large, white, rectangular home surrounded by several barns and outbuildings. An empty buggy sat just to the side of the house. Between the buggy and the house, black trousers and blue, cotton dresses flapped on a clothesline in the gentle breeze. The front door squeaked on its hinges as a woman in blue stepped out on the porch. She came down the steps, black shoes and black stockings below her aproned dress, one hand reaching up to tuck a gray strand of hair beneath her white bonnet.

"Have you come for berries?" She smiled as she spoke in her clipped, German accent.

Tom stepped slightly forward. "Yes, we would like to pick."

"Come with me. I'll show you where to start. We haven't had many people from town."

"How do you know we're from town?" Tom asked.

"Well," she said with a twinkle in her eye, "if you were from around here, I would know you."

Tom turned and pointed toward the house, where ten rocking chairs stretched from one side of the front porch to the other like bent old men, rigidly poised, listening for the call to dinner. "You must get a lot of company; there are so many rockers."

She turned back toward the porch, shaded her eyes, and spoke as if she could see someone we couldn't. "I raised ten boys. We needed a lot of chairs. I miss my children, but they come to visit and bring their families, so we still need all those rocking chairs."

"Weren't you glad to marry off that many boys?" Tom teased.

She turned and faced us with a mother's love etched on her features. "Oh, it was so much more fun to add a plate to the table when each one was born than to take away a plate when one got married and left home."

In the quiet presence of this loving mother, we walked to the rows of berries. She waved her arm. "Pick as many as you like. Stop at the house when you are done, and we will settle up."

Tom and I picked quickly in the beginning. But, as the sun beat on our backs and the thorns pricked our fingers, we slowed down.

I noticed Tom eating one now and then. "Hey, buddy," I said "put 'em in the boxes. I don't want to be out here all day."

"My boxes are getting full!" he insisted.

We worked through lunch, wiping the sweat from our foreheads as we carried cardboard boxes of berries back to our car. Early in the afternoon, we paid our bill, slid into the hot seat of our Ford Maverick, fastened our seat belts, and drove down the dusty road toward home. Tom carried the berries into the house while I started washing and bagging. The Ziploc bags full of sugared berries would go into the freezer for pies or fruit salads or just for snacks.

A moaning came from the couch, where Tom was stretched out with his hands on his stomach.

"What's wrong with you?" I exclaimed. "There are fifty million berries here; you can't quit now."

Tom moaned more loudly. "I can't. I'm sick! I ate too many!"

Exasperated, I said, "Hey, I'm not doing all these by myself!"

"You'll have to. I'm really sick. I've never eaten so many red raspberries in my life. They were so good, I couldn't stop."

"Tom Anderson! How old are you? I can't believe that a twenty-five-year-old medical student would eat so many raspberries that he couldn't get up off the couch. You should know better."

"I know. But my stomach hurts so much. I don't want to move."

I walked to the couch and tried to roll him off, "C'mon! You are not getting out of this."

He rolled toward the inside of the couch and moaned even more loudly. "Please, let me just lie here. I promise I won't ever do it again. But, right now, I don't even want to look at those berries." I finished the berries that day and never let him know how hard it was to hide my laughter. There were plenty of other opportunities for Tom to help with garden produce or acquired fruit. A Mennonite farmer, who had become a good friend of ours, gave us half an acre of ground where we grew our own food. It was only a short drive from our apartment. With Tom's green thumb, we planted beans, sweet potatoes, broccoli, tomatoes, spinach, and butternut squash. After classes, we drove our little Maverick to our garden plot and hauled a trunk-load of garden produce back to the apartment. One day, we spent hours leaning over the side of the bathtub, washing spinach leaves. Tomatoes got turned into spaghetti sauce and soup or canned whole for chili. At night, after studying, we sat at the kitchen table and peeled all the tiny sweet potatoes that we knew would spoil over the winter. The big potatoes would get eaten first, but we crammed the little ones into jars and preserved them for the winter months.

Our butternut squash produced a bumper crop. We cooked them, peeled them, and stuffed them into bags for the freezer. By the end of the first year, we were pretty sure our skin had an orange cast to it after consuming so many sweet potatoes and butternut squash. With the broccoli, we made soup, soufflé, stir-fry, and cheesy broccoli. For having no income, we ate a very healthy diet. As we learned to survive by preserving our own meat, fruit, and vegetables, we felt like we fulfilled Grant Wood's *American Gothic* . We were living examples of the determined-to-survive, independent spirit he had captured in that painting.

Not only did we have plenty of food for ourselves, but we often prepared meals for friends. Our apartment was tiny, but it was frequently full of friends, food, and fellowship. While Tom's parents were in New York, we used their Jenny Lind-style sofa so they didn't have to put it in storage. But, the rest of our apartment décor included Tom's Coca-Cola collection of tin pictures, an old icebox, a cast-iron stove, a bookcase made out of barn siding with a rattlesnake skin hanging on the side, a stuffed owl perched on part of a branch suspended from the wall, and his old oak schoolteacher's desk. It was a crowded little abode, but it didn't stop us from having fun with friends and family.

Tom worked hard at home and harder still at school. His efforts did not go unnoticed. After working for several months at the pulmonary unit in the hospital, his evaluation read:

> Mr. Anderson's performance was rated above average. All who came in contact with him commented on his intensity, hard work, and ability to work with others. He showed great concern for his patients, even tracking down one discharged patient at the bus station to give him some medication the patient had

left behind. He has the attributes and abilities to be an excellent physician and all are confident that he will attain such status.

Although Tom had two more years of medical school in Iowa, I completed my bachelor's degree in the summer of 1980, while being the only woman on campus who was nine months pregnant. Six days after I received my diploma, we drove to our garden to weed the spinach.

I never knew for sure if it was the thought of getting on my hands and knees in the hot August sun and weeding the garden or if it really was "my time," but I put my hands on my very large tummy and said, "Tom, I've never been in labor before, but I'm pretty sure we need to go to the hospital."

Tom hurried me into the care, and he flew over the country roads, grabbed my bags at the apartment, and skidded to a stop at the emergency-room entrance of the hospital. Twenty-three hours later, the delivery room nurse handed Tom his first child, a beautiful baby girl. Tom always said she cooed like a dove in the delivery room. In every way, she was perfect.

There was no father more proud than Tom. He ran to K-mart and bought her a blue-and-white-striped dress with a little yellow duck on the front. After he brought us home from the hospital and settled into our apartment, he disappeared for about an hour. When he came back, he carried two grocery bags full of stuffed animals that he had purchased from the local Goodwill store. He wanted his little girl to have everything a child ought to have.

In the evenings, when he came home from classes, he wrapped his baby girl in a Snugli carrier that fit over his shoulders and around his stomach. In the Snugli, he took her for a walk while I fixed supper.

When we went to the fiddlers' picnic in October, Tom carried his little girl to the hillside at the edge of town, where the musicians played and people sat on blankets on the grass. If we

went to The Mill, she went with us. When we picked apples from
a local orchard for applesauce and cider, he carried her.

December 25 was nearing, and we both wanted a tree for
our little girl's first Christmas, but we didn't have the money.
Tom drove up and down country roads until he found a five-
foot tree with bare branches growing in a ditch. Jumping out,
he cut the tree with his hand-saw and shoved it in the car. We
propped the tree up in our living room and decorated it with one
cord of lights, leaving the bird's nest that came with it in the top
branch. Thirty years later, two friends from our Iowa City days,
who later became physicians, said they never forgot walking into
our apartment and seeing that tree. A lot of Christmases have
come and gone, but they remembered our little tree as the most
beautiful one they ever saw.

Tom continued his studies while I stayed home with our
daughter and cared for another little boy whose mother was on
staff at the medical school. The thirty-five dollars a week we
received for his care covered the few groceries we bought from
the store. The boy's mother, who was the Associate for Student
Affairs, wrote one of Tom's recommendations for his application
to residency.

> I am happy to be asked to recommend Tom Anderson
> for a residency in family practice. I have known Tom
> in two capacities, student and husband/father. As a
> medical student, he has been outstanding in academics
> and extra-curricular [activities].
>
> Since I have had daily contact with the Andersons, I
> feel qualified to comment on Tom as a husband and
> father, a role which he takes very seriously. His wife
> has taken care of my fifteen-month-old son twenty-
> five hours each week in their home. . . . .

Tom is an actively involved husband and father. He is forthright and caring. Not only do I recommend Tom most highly to your program, but also his family to your community. They are an extremely able, solid, and tender people.

Our lives were very full. It was the summer before Tom's last year of medical school when I said, "Tom, I'm pretty sure our little girl is going to have a brother or sister."

Her little brother came into the world with the blizzard of March 1, 1982. At Tom's medical-school graduation day in May that year, he proudly held his daughter in one arm and his son in the other. These were good years and happy years, full of experiences that would fortify us for the times to come.

CHAPTER 5

FROM MUNCIE TO HOME

"WE-E-ELL," SHE DRAWLED IT OUT, "my momma is from Tennessee, my pappy is from Tennessee, and I'm from Tennessee too. Ain't never been any place but Tennessee or right here in Muncie, Indiana. I've got a baby, and I don't s'pose he'll ever go anywhere a'tall."

The young beautician leaned back and looked with a practiced eye at my hair. Picking up a strand of hair, she snipped, and looked critically at the ends. "Looks pretty darn good to me. You just get on back here, sweet pea, if yore not happy with yer cut."

I slid out of the chair, picked up my purse, and paid at the register, leaving a nice tip for Miss Tennessee. I had asked her where she was from when I heard her accent, but I knew already that she was another one of the imports from the hills of Tennessee to the town of Muncie, Indiana.

After Tom's graduation from medical school, we loaded a U-Haul, piled the children in the car, and moved to Muncie for his three years of family practice residency. Tom had wanted a program that would prepare him for a rural community and at the same time, not place his family in a major city. On his application for residency, he had written,

When I take a moment to reflect on what I really value in life, I realize that I could be without many material things and still be quite happy as long as I could hold onto two things: life itself and my family. I value and cherish my family dearly. Without it, I would experience a deep void that could never be completely filled by other things. I believe that there are many people who feel the same way I do. However, I find that in today's society, the continued existence of the family as an ideal is threatened. Today, the family receives little support from society.

I have chosen family practice as a specialty for many reasons. But, one of the most important reasons is because I believe it will allow me to help support and preserve the family in today's society. In today's fractionated sub-specialized medicine, I feel that the family physician plays a vital role in being one of the few health care providers who can truly deliver comprehensive care. By being able to provide care for all the members of a family, the family physician has a unique opportunity to see and help meet the special needs of the family, and thus help to support and preserve the family as an ideal in today's society.

I have had the opportunity to live in both rural Illinois and Indiana, and also to live in the urbanized world of Chicago. Each situation has its unique attributes; however, I have found that my family and I are best suited for rural living. Therefore, my career plans are rural family practice. I hope to settle near either my wife's family farm in Indiana, or my family farm in Illinois, and practice medicine in one of the nearby communities.

Muncie, sprawled out in the flat, eastern farmland of Indiana, was the home of Ball Memorial Hospital, Tom's choice for his family practice residency. The city had an interesting contrast of people. Some of them came from Tennessee to work in the Ball jar factory in one part of town, while on the other side of town, Ball State University campus swarmed with students. It didn't matter which side of town you were visiting, people were friendly.

The best thing about residency for a young doctor was that he or she actually received a paycheck after four years of college, followed by four years of medical school with no money. Tom's starting salary in 1982 was sixteen thousand dollars a year. It paid the rent on our three-bedroom home in the new housing addition at the edge of town, but didn't leave a whole lot of money left over. The first thing we did was install a woodstove to combat the expense of an all-electric home. Then we tore up the lovely suburban backyard and planted the only garden in the whole housing addition. That pretty much took care of our heating bill and food costs. We shopped garage sales and Goodwill stores for clothing and house furnishings.

Tom and I became members of St. Andrew's Presbyterian Church in Muncie, where both of our children were baptized. Although Tom participated as a deacon, it was very hard to be involved in church fellowship with the rigorous schedule of residency. Many hours were spent in the hospital, learning from other physicians and residents as well as learning how to manage complicated patients. There were nights Tom would come home later than usual because he had given an indigent person a ride home from the emergency room. Other times he came home with an extra mouth to feed. He could never turn his back on a person in need.

Although most residents were consumed by hospital demands, Tom needed outside interests to keep him sane. He enrolled in a pottery class at the university and took up beekeeping. He kept the beehives at my parents' farm, which was only a couple of hours away from Muncie.

Before going to the hospital one morning, Tom was drinking coffee with me in our living room. He looked over the top of the newspaper he was reading and announced, "They are going to have a seminar next week on transcendental meditation. I think I should go. I've heard people say that it really helps with relaxation."

"Hmmm. Are you having trouble relaxing?" I asked.

"Yeah, sometimes I get so wound up. I have tried reading the Psalms and praying, but it seems like it's really hard to slow my mind down. I worry a lot about my patients, whether I've missed something or have done the right procedure. I don't want to drink alcohol, but I need some way to help me relax."

"I don't know if transcendental meditation is a good choice. I've read about it, and it seems to have pros and cons. Why don't you pray about going?" I suggested, inwardly concerned about the spiritual source of transcendental meditation.

Several days went by before the night of the seminar arrived. Tom left after supper to attend the meeting. I prayed fervently for his protection and his ability to judge wisely the value of the subject matter. A short time later, after both children were in bed, I heard Tom's car in the driveway. He walked in the front door, tossed his keys on the table, kicked off his shoes, and flopped down on the couch.

"Well?" I asked.

"That was the most ridiculous thing I've ever attended. I left after thirty minutes." He sighed, stretching out on his stomach.

"I'll give you a back rub," I said, bending over and starting with his shoulders, much relieved by his decision.

Stress is an inescapable element in the practice of medicine. Assuming the health-care responsibility for real people and making life-and-death decisions weighs on every conscientious resident. They know that one day soon, they will be on their own. That day came so quickly for Tom. He had worked hard as a resident. He also had taken a second job in a near-by emergency room, learned how to mold Japanese pottery, and maintained his beehives on the farm while gleaning everything he could from his training program. One of the most important lessons Tom took away from his residency was a piece of advice from Dr. Phil Ball. "If you listen to your patients, Tom, they will diagnose themselves most of the time," he said as the two of them worked together one afternoon. "You see, many doctors begin to think they have had all this education so they know more than their patients. But nobody knows their own body as well as the patient does. Listen carefully to what they tell you."

When Tom eventually established his own practice, one of the attributes he became known for was his diagnostic skill. He did listen to his patients, and he cared deeply about each one.

At the end of residency, we needed to decide where Tom would practice and where we would settle permanently. Finally, we could stop moving! Surprisingly, Tom was more adamant than I was about where we should live. His mother called to tell us that she had found two positions available for him, but he said we were going home … to my parents' farm.

In the spring of 1985, we made our last move together. My parents sold us their old brick farm-house and twenty acres surrounding it, while they purchased a near-by farm. At last, we were surrounded by farmland, woods, and rural people.

Just a half mile away from our new home, three elderly bachelor brothers lived in the house where they had been raised on the top of a wooded hill. Tom loved to visit these brothers, who sat around their potbelly stove in the winter.

"Hey, Tom," one of them said on a blustery January day, "have you ever been up in one of those airplanes?"

"Well, actually, several times. I like to fly because it gets me where I need to go quickly. How about you boys? You ever been in a plane?"

The "boys" got excited, as one of them explained, "Yes, we did ride in an airplane. It was just once. It was one of those small planes that didn't go far. We got way up over the fields."

Another one interrupted. "We could see everything. You can't believe what was in plain sight from up there. We even saw the state lines. No kidding!"

One cloudy day in summer, the brothers explained to Tom how to know if it was going to rain, "You have to go down by the barn. C'mon, we'll show you."

They hoisted up their overalls, put on their barn boots, and walked through the grass that never got mowed by any machine. Sheep wandered the hillside and ate their fill. Nearing the barn, the three brothers abruptly stopped. One of them pointed toward the ground and said, "See that big rock poking its head out right there. You come down here any day, and if that rock starts to sweat, you know it's going to rain in the next twenty-four hours."

It was good to be home. We planted a garden twice the size we'd ever had, and we bought a red Vermont Castings woodstove. We bought dairy goats for milk, sheep for meat, chickens for eggs, and dairy calves for extra meat and income. Fruit trees and a grape arbor had already been well-established by my parents. We settled in with two ecstatic children and bought a fluffy, white Great Pyrenees guard dog for the livestock. Our son wanted to name it Salt, but we settled on Sugar.

Although Tom's training and heart was in family practice, he wasn't ready to commit himself to the tremendous responsibility of caring for a community or to bear the financial burden of setting up a private practice. Like most students, Tom had accumulated a considerable debt from the expense of medical school. He took a job in the emergency room so we could pay his college loans and buy the necessary provisions for our new homestead. However, the erratic hours of the emergency-room schedule wreaked havoc with Tom's sleep patterns and with our daily life. To keep the house quiet after Tom worked all night, I would load the children in the car and take them to the park for hours.

For this reason, Tom soon switched from the emergency room to an urgent-care position. The urgent-care facility closed at 11:00 p.m., so he was able to quit working the long night hours. Even if it was almost midnight when he arrived home, he was able to be in bed at night and awake during daylight hours. After a year, Tom left the urgent care position for another opportunity. The nursing staff gave him a packet of awards on his last day, which included these honors:

> A Scholarship Award - to the Catholic school of your choice for a refresher course in penmanship, as only the nuns can teach it.

> The Maybe They Won't Notice I'm Suturing Award - for having the outstanding ability to relax a patient by talking about everything from 2 X 4's to combines. (If we weren't ladies, we'd call this good BS.)

> The Most Faithful Husband of the Year Award - for choosing lobster over sexual favors and for being able to resist the sex kitten in curlers, off-the-shoulder nightie, and lying on the floor.

> The Nike Award - for the most miles walked in a single hallway.

> The Urgent Care Most Sadly Missed Ever Award - for being the best Doctor any of us could ever hope to work with. We'll miss you.

Tom knew there was "something more" for him to do, but he wasn't ready for it yet. He would fill one more position before finding his niche.

CHAPTER 6

FIRED

TOM REALIZED FROM HIS TIME in urgent care that he wanted to be more involved in his patients' on-going treatment. But he was still reluctant to commit himself to practicing medicine in a rural community. He knew that he would want to take care of his own patients, and that would mean being available for emergencies day and night. He also knew it would mean the financial investment of purchasing equipment and an office. To open his own practice would require stamina, commitment, availability, and a large financial expenditure. With a growing family, it was a risk Tom wasn't sure he should take. So, when a position in occupational medicine opened up, he applied. In the late eighties, occupational medicine was still developing as an area of its own. For Tom, it was an opportunity to start on the ground floor of a relatively new field and creatively develop care, treatment, and preventive strategies for a community of employees. By the time our second son was born, Tom was the on-site physician for the Subaru-Isuzu plant in Lafayette, Indiana.

Very quickly, Tom realized the personal, internal conflicts this position involved. After a year of treating carpel tunnel syndrome resulting from repetitious wrist movements on the production line, he was discouraged. "This isn't a good way for me to practice medicine," he admitted in frustration. "I wish I could develop more programs for rehabilitation, and I wish I could implement the use of robotic equipment in the plant. I'm not able to help anyone in a permanent way.

"What do you think, Tom?" I asked. "Maybe it's time to do what you've always wanted to do. You trained in family medicine, and I have a feeling you will really enjoy it. If you don't, something else will open up."

Tom longed to care for the family unit, but for him, it was a tremendous responsibility. When he graduated from medical school, he and his classmates swore to uphold "an oath that bears the name of Hippocrates," which is a form of the original Hippocratic Oath sworn to by physicians throughout the centuries.

> I do solemnly swear by that which I hold most sacred:
>
> That I will be loyal to the profession of medicine and just and generous to it members;
>
> That I will lead my life and practice my art in uprightness and honor;
>
> That into whatsoever house I shall enter, it shall be for the good of the sick to the utmost of my power, holding myself aloof from wrong, from corruption, and from the temptation of others to vice;
>
> That I will exercise my art solely for the cure of my patients, and will give no drug, perform no operation for a criminal purpose, even if solicited, and far less suggest such a thing.

That whatsoever I shall see or hear of the lives of my patients which is not fitting to be spoken, I will keep inviolably secret.

These things I do promise, and in proportion as I am faithful to this, my oath, may happiness and good repute be ever mine - the opposite if I shall be forsworn.

Tom took this oath very seriously as he practiced in the emergency room, urgent care, and occupational medicine, but he knew it was even more relevant when caring for families in a community. The responsibility intimidated him. But, he also knew that his heart was in family medicine. In 1993, he left his position at the Subaru-Isuzu plant, much to the chagrin of many employees, and joined a family practice clinic in a near-by town. Many farm families and rural people along with the approximately three thousand town residents utilized the clinic. The two-physician facility was part of a larger medical complex in Lafayette. As the patients came, he knew that he had made a move in the right direction.

Some of the farm people he grew to love dearly belonged to a local religious sect often referred to as "the horse-and-buggy people." They had other official names, but most locals knew them as the horse-and-buggy folks. People outside the community assumed they were Amish. They looked Amish, but their sect was doctrinally different from the Amish.

Our horse-and-buggy people worked with their hands on the land or in their private shop; they had no electricity, although they did use gas lamps; they rode bicycles or drove a horse with a cart or buggy; and most of them had large families. The men generally wore blue shirts with black pants and suspenders, and black, broad-brimmed hats or straw ones in the summer. The women wore bonnets, long-sleeved dresses with capes, and usually dark stockings and shoes.

Tom came home one day and announced, "I want to join the horse-and-buggy church."

"Really?" I asked, surprised. "Why would you want to do that?"

"I love their families. I love the way they take care of their elderly, and I like the simplicity of their lifestyle. They focus on the important things: serving God and one another. They don't complicate their lives or their church. Let's go worship with them this Sunday.

We did. We took our three children and parked our car in the parking lot with all the horses and buggies. Among the black capes, black jackets, and black hats, we wound our way to the back pew of the little, wood-framed church. From the back, the men were all sitting on the left side of the room while all the women sat to the right side. Children sat on both sides under the supervision of their parents. There was no air-conditioning in summer or furnace in winter, but the woodstove sizzled. There was no choir or electronic devices - not even a pulpit. There was a table with elders and deacons surrounding it and wooden pews for the congregation. From the Bible, the word of God was taught by one of the elders. Singing was slower than we were accustomed to. Each verse was read out loud then sung with a very slow, drawn-out, nasal intonation. If the congregation was singing "Fairest Lord Jesus," you could start on "Fairest," slip out to the outhouse, and make it back in time for Jesus. It wasn't bad singing, just different.

After the two-hour service, we adjourned for dinner. One of the families invited us to their home. Sunday dinner was tender roast, creamy mashed potatoes, buttered vegetables, homemade bread, fruit preserved from summer, and an assortment of pies with flaky crusts. The visiting with each other and the discussion of the morning sermon continued into the late afternoon while children played games and babies slept.

When we finally left for home, Tom asked, "Don't you just love them?"

"Tom," I teased, "I think you always wanted to be Amish. This is your chance."

"Seriously," he insisted, "one of the things I like about them is that the men take responsibility to be the head of their household, and they also take responsibility to lead in the church. Today, men fail to lead their families spiritually, and too many women run our churches, not that women don't have a lot to contribute - they do. But men sit back and don't become the role models and protectors that they should be."

For several months, we attended the little country church. In preparation for joining, Tom bought two draft horses and a buggy. Finally, he had an opportunity to speak with the elder of the church. He explained to Tom that they believed in working the land and providing for their households with the labor from their own hands. A college degree and a medical practice was a departure from their customs and traditions. To take on membership and the horse-and-buggy lifestyle was not their recommendation for him. However, he would always be lovingly welcomed to fellowship with them. This decision was a little hard for Tom to accept at the time, but later he could see God's wisdom and protection in steering him down a different road.

As a second choice, Tom became a member of the German Baptist Church that was also thriving in our county. Their church format was similar to the horse-and-buggy community, as was their attire, but they allowed their members to drive cars, use electricity, and have modern conveniences.

One of the first times we attended a service, I wore a cherry-red down coat. When we entered with our family, many heads turned, and children stared over the back of the pews. Everyone wore black winter coats or capes. As we slid into the car after the service, I told Tom, "Okay, the cherry-red coat is going to have to go. I felt like a prostitute at a prayer meeting."

Tom laughed. "Nah, you look good in red. I like your coat. Besides, you're not buying a new coat because you're afraid of what someone thinks about it. If the Holy Spirit tells you to get a different coat, then you can buy one."

Tom's membership in the German Baptist Church did not go unnoticed in our rural community. After joining the church, he dressed like the rest of the German Baptist brethren. His pants had no zipper, but buttoned on each side, and his black suspenders and brushed-back, "bowl-cut" hair stood out at hospital functions and other gatherings. Colleagues were quick to tease him about his new look and about "joining church." Some chiding drifted toward me.

As I was walking down the road one day, a man slowed his truck, pulled over and asked, "So, what's it like to sleep with an Amish man?"

"Just as good as sleeping with him before he was Amish," I responded, as I continued to walk.

When I told Tom about it later, he laughed uproariously, as did I. We figured if there were an underground newspaper for local gossip, we had unintentionally made the front page.

Tom was thoroughly enjoying the people in his practice by this time, but he was deeply troubled by the fees charged to his patients. One day, he commented to a patient about the "price gouging" that he felt was being done. Word got back to the administrator of the clinic that Tom had accused them of being greedy and of charging unreasonable fees. He was given twenty-four hours to resign.

At home, with my hands in the dish water, I heard the phone ring. Oblivious to the crisis Tom was in, I dried my hands and answered with a cheery "hello?"

"I just got fired." Tom's voice was on the edge of panic.

"What? What are you talking about?" I asked in disbelief.

"Well, not fired, but basically fired. I was told to resign if I didn't want to be fired."

"What happened?" I asked with alarm.

He talked fast, and I could hear the strain in his voice. "I said the clinic is price gouging their patients. For instance, a common thyroid test only costs about fourteen dollars, but patients are billed around a hundred dollars. Costs don't have to be that high. Word got back to the administrator that I am criticizing them. He wants me gone … today!"

"But, that's crazy," I argued. "You're such a good doctor. Why would they want to lose you?"

"I don't know, but I have to clean out my office right now. Can you bring the truck and help me load my stuff? Everything has to be out of here before tomorrow morning."

"I'll be right there," I promised.

"I don't know what we are going to do!" he exclaimed.

"Hey, Tom, you're a very good physician. You'll get work. Don't worry, okay?"

I hung up and ran to our farm truck. It was a 1978 Ford, about which I stubbornly told people, "It starts every time I turn the key, and it's paid for." There were quite a few dents, no tailgate, and rusted sides, but it did start. I barreled down the road into town. Pulling up to the back door of the medical office, I met Tom coming out with a box full of his belongings.

Sliding out of the truck cab, I hurried to him. "You okay?" I asked.

"Let's just get this stuff loaded," he said with a tired look.

We shoved boxes, crates, pictures, office chairs, personal equipment, and other paraphernalia into our truck. I drove it home, with Tom following behind. It was a gloomy, sullen atmosphere that evening around the supper table. Tom knew by then that he loved taking care of families; he longed to be a part of whole-family medical care. But, after resigning, it was impossible for him to practice in a five-county perimeter due to a clause written into every physician's contract. The restrictive clause could be negated by paying a fee of two hundred thousand dollars, which we did not have.

We decided to take a much-needed vacation. Piling into our Buick Park Avenue, we headed west with our children and our camping gear in tow. We rolled through the northern plains until we reached Glacier National Park in Montana. We pitched our family-sized tent and camped, hiked the trails, ate buffalo burgers, and drank mountain huckleberry milkshakes.

While the children slept, Tom and I sat by the campfire. With my shoe, I gently nudged his foot. "What are you thinking?"

"I'm worried. I need to take care of my family. I have failed to provide. I've lost my job. You want to know more?" he asked with despair.

"You'll find a job," I assured him. "I think you're looking for something else, Tom."

"What? What do you mean?" he asked, surprised.

"Well, think about it. The church in Chicago was like a family. The-horse and-buggy community and the German Baptist group were both very much like an extended family. I'm here. Your children are here. But you're searching for an extended family relationship that you don't have with your biological relatives."

Tom was quiet for a minute before answering. "Okay, Miss Know-it-all, maybe I am. You don't know what it's like to be estranged from your family."

After our marriage and the birth of our children, Tom and I failed to mend the growing rift with his parents. Was it our fault or their fault or a combination of both? Was it our immaturity or was it a succession of misunderstandings that left each side with wounded feelings? Even with hindsight, it's hard to discern the answers. But the result was that our rocky relationship with his parents also affected our relationship with two of his other three siblings. Tom struggled with a tremendous void of familial ties throughout his life. As the years passed, I noticed that especially as the Thanksgiving and Christmas holidays approached, he often sank into a silent depression. In the early years, I would ask, "What is it?"

He struggled to define the cause. "I guess I feel like I don't have a family, except for my oldest brother. Sometimes I don't even know if my parents love me. Maybe they never did."

"Tom, I think they loved you as much as they were able, but I think we are each bound by our own limitations in how well we can express love. Some of us are a lot more limited than others by the burdens we carry through life."

With pained, questioning eyes, he asked, "Why didn't my dad protect me? I wanted him to fight for me. I wanted somebody to come to my defense. My parents knew the man who molested me, but they continued to be friends with him. Why? Why didn't anybody care what was happening to me?"

"I don't know, Tom," I admitted, sadly.

"My parents knew that I was being molested. They allowed the man to spend time with me again and again. He molested me repeatedly. I don't know how to have a relationship with parents who would allow that. My family exists, but we're not a family."

As we sat around the campfire, I reached over and took my husband's hand. "God designed the human race in family units, Tom. It is probably very normal for you to try to fill the void left by your parents and siblings. Just don't forget the family that you do have. We love you very much, and we need you."

"I'd rather be dead than hurt you guys in any way," he said firmly.

"Well, you're not hurting us. I mean, look at the things we've learned: we can all hitch a horse and drive a team now; we have learned how to make hominy from field corn with the horse-and-buggy people; we've made so many interesting friends from different plain (a general term for any Anabaptist church group) communities. Most of all, we've learned to find Jesus in the midst of different cultures and traditions. I think we're doing just fine."

"So, what are we going to do now? I have no job." He sighed, and his shoulders slumped.

"You have no job because you have integrity and a tender heart," I insisted, "not because you aren't intelligent, capable, or hardworking."

"Let's go home, tomorrow," he said. "I'm not going to have any peace of mind until I find employment."

"What are the stipulations of the contract?" I asked.

"I can't work in the county where I resigned, nor can I work in any contiguous county."

"Okay. So what are our options? We need a place just across the county line where your patients can still find you but you can't get penalized. What about the old meat market in Clymers?" I asked, excitedly.

Clymers was a little burg with no more than a dozen or so houses. Right next to the highway in Clymers, a wood-framed building with cement flower boxes in front had a hand-written *For Sale* sign in the yard. We had always suspected it might be a place for selling illegal drugs, since it seemed an unlikely place to purchase meat, but it was easily accessed. In recent months, the building had been empty.

"Hey," Tom said, thoughtfully, "that just might work. Do you want to start driving home tonight? I'm wide awake."

"Why not?" I said, standing up. "The kids can sleep while we drive. Let's pack up and go."

We cleaned our campground site and drove east through the night. We were going to transform a meat market into a medical office.

CHAPTER 7

THE CHIROPRACTOR, THE MEAT MARKET, AND THE DEPOT

BY THE TIME WE RETURNED home, word had spread that Tom was out of a job and out of a place to practice medicine. One of his elderly patients heard that the building in Clymers was available, and he handed Tom the twenty-five thousand dollars in cash that he needed to buy the building. It was a no-interest loan to be paid back when the practice was able to provide the income. Another friend and patient, who was a chiropractor in Logansport, a town seven miles from Clymers, offered us his office as a temporary practice site. He used his office during the day, so it became Dr. Anderson's medical office from five to nine o'clock in the evening while we renovated the old meat building.

Fortunately, Tom had decided that we should home-school our children. This meant books, videos, and school hours during days at home, and it also meant our children had more free time in the evenings. With no income, staffing our temporary office was not an option. Tom worked on the Clymers office during the day and then loaded his family in the car every evening, and each member took on the role of receptionist, nurse, or record keeper. Only our youngest son was allowed to play with the toys in the waiting room. The rest of us worked.

As Tom's nursing assistant, I helped gather patients' histories or complaints and got them ready to see the doctor. I always had to be available when Tom did pap smears or other private exams. One evening, I carefully helped a female patient stretch out on the chiropractor's bed and get ready for her pap test. The beds were designed differently from those in a medical facility. Each bed had more movable parts to assist a chiropractor in his adjustments. I helped the woman get situated comfortably just as Tom came into the room and greeted her. Suddenly, the bed slid apart and down went the woman's bottom. Tom and I both tried to catch her. It was awkward, but the three of us ended up sitting on the floor, laughing hysterically.

Every evening, the patient schedule was full. When we loaded up the portable medical equipment, turned the rooms back into a chiropractor's office, and headed home, we were all tired.

In the meantime, Tom worked to transform the meat market into a medical facility. Whether drugs had really been swapped out at the building, we never knew for sure. It didn't matter. For all practical purposes, it was a meat market that desperately needed a face-lift.

When we first walked in the front door, a gigantic black-and-white Holstein cow painted on particle board greeted us. Unused meat counters and empty refrigerator units cluttered the main room. Everything had to be gutted. We were blessed by kind people and caring patients; many volunteers came to work on the building. Carpenters and drywall men came from the German Baptist Church. Plumbers and electricians showed up. Horse-and-buggy people hitched rides to lend their hands. Friends and family pitched in to paint and decorate.

As a legitimate medical office began to rise out of the rubble, Tom needed to acquire personnel to staff the new facility. One of the women he hired was Rosanna. Years later, she wrote a letter to me about her work experience with Tom.

> I first met Dr. Anderson as a patient. I was immediately drawn to the compassion and care he showed. He really listened to what I was telling him, and then he gave his opinion and medical care.
>
> At that time, he mentioned that he wanted to start his own practice. I told him to remember me if he did start on his own, since I loved the medical field. He called me, and I started working for him at Clymers, in March 1994. The building was a very simple one, but due to Dr. Anderson's care, there was soon a thriving practice underway.
>
> Dr. Anderson very patiently taught us, his staff, everything we needed to know. We had no pre-conceived ideas, so we did things his way. Most of the time, his way involved old-fashioned, cost-saving principles that made the patient's well-being a priority. If a patient wanted to try natural medicine, it was fine with him. As long as he could help you get well, he would do whatever got results.
>
> Dr. Anderson could always make us and the patients laugh. He would never laugh at you, but with you. For instance, sometimes a female patient would need a pessary, which is a medical device used to treat uterine prolapse or urinary incontinence. Not being professionally trained, we girls thought he was saying "piss area" instead of pessary. He only had to correct us one time! We all laughed!

More and more people heard of Dr. Anderson's perception and correct diagnosing. Watching him practice was awe-inspiring. His brilliant mind was always on target, and if he had questions, he always called someone for advice.

He had compassion for everyone, but he especially loved helping babies and the elderly. When he did minor office surgery, we loved helping him. The wonderful stories he could tell soon had people laughing and at ease about the procedure at hand. This very gifted doctor was not afraid to tackle any challenge, but he also knew when a specialist was needed.

Who can forget the lady patient who loved ballroom dancing? Dr. Anderson took her in his arms, swung her around the waiting room, dipped her low, and proceeded to fall on top of her. We all laughed hysterically.

Regardless of their ailment, patients always left feeling better than when they came.

Clymers is an unremarkable small town on the side of the highway in the middle of nowhere. But, for two years, it entertained the hustle and bustle of a thriving medical practice. As the two years of forced exile came to a close, Tom began to look for an office in Camden, Indiana. We found an old train depot that was perfect. Once again, the money was handed to us from a loving patient to purchase the depot. Both loans were rapidly paid back as Tom's practice continued to grow; but the kindness and generosity was never forgotten. Surely, God used the hands and help of many to guide us along the way.

Turning a depot into an office building became another community project. As the practice was steadily increasing, Tom hired a registered nurse from one of his previous jobs in Lafayette. She sent him this note:

"I want you to know how very proud and happy it makes me that you want to continue our association in your new career. You couldn't pay me any higher compliment than to take me with you. Even if it doesn't work out that I can go, it was that you asked that mattered to me. You're a great doctor and one of the kindest men I know. You have earned my loyalty and respect by the example you set. I pray I never let you down. I stand a little straighter when someone says, "Oh, you work for Dr. Anderson.""

The staff increased, the patients increased, and our quiver of arrows at home increased. Our children were now ages fifteen, thirteen, and six. After the last son, we had agreed that I would have a tubal ligation done. Tom and I were both thirty-five. During the following years, as we home-schooled our children and watched God work in our family as well as in Tom's professional life, we wondered about the contemporary use of birth control. We didn't question whether it was right or wrong; we questioned whether an area such as childbearing might not be an important issue to discuss with our heavenly Father before resorting to birth control. With our modern technology and hectic lives, it was assumed, perhaps presumptuously, that we would automatically know the best size for our family and the perfect timing for each birth. Shouldn't this be something to pray about? We did pray. And even though we were both forty years old when we made the decision, we decided to have a tubal reversal performed.

The doctor doing the reversal said that a sperm count from the father needed to be done because if the number of live sperm wasn't high enough, they wouldn't do the procedure. It would be a waste of the patient's money.

"Did you do the test?" I kept asking Tom.

Finally, he admitted, "Okay, look, I did the test. I'm getting old. If I turn in those results, they will never do the operation. So I'm going to tell them I forgot to bring the results with me, but I will say the numbers are just fine. This is something you and I feel God wants us to do, so we will just do it and take full responsibility."

We went through with the surgery at the end of March. In July, I called the doctor with the news that I was going to have a baby. She shouted through the phone in disbelief, "You're kidding! Oh, my gosh, that is your miracle baby!"

Because Tom was self-employed in a solo practice and medical coverage was so expensive, we carried a policy that would not cover much of the hospital delivery expense. Tom and I decided we would do the unthinkable and have a home delivery since I had already given birth to three healthy babies with no problems. It would have been an unremarkable delivery except that at the last minute Tom realized the bed was a little low.

He turned and grabbed a black beanbag chair. "Here, sit on this."

"Are you crazy? I'm not delivering a baby on a beanbag chair!" I said indignantly between breaths.

"Just do it! I need you to be higher so I can catch the baby," he said, trying to shove the beanbag beneath me.

"Maybe you should have thought of that sooner!" I gasped between contractions as Tom lifted me.

On April 20, 1995, at age forty-one, Tom delivered his last child, a child born out of faith and obedience. We named her Lily, because, like the lilies of the field, we had trusted God for her. She was beautiful and perfect. And, yes, she was born on a beanbag chair, which her older siblings never let her forget.

Not only had God blessed us with a baby, but He also had brought us to a church home. Being part of the local German Baptist Church community, we met many brothers and sisters who became lifelong friends. However, because of Tom's disagreement with some of the doctrinal statements of the church, he had to be excluded from membership. Once again, he sought out the horse-and-buggy community for fellowship.

But God had a different plan. He sent Herman. Herman lived in Nappanee, Indiana, and was a member of the Old Brethren Church. His church was one of the different sects among the plain community. Herman had heard about Tom and came looking for him. The father of eight children and eventually sixty-some grandchildren, Herman didn't know how *not* to preach the gospel. Everything he did or said was to bring people to Jesus. His whole philosophy on being a Christian was wrapped up in the following poem given to Tom from one of his patients. The authors signed only with their initials: A. J. F. and A. O. S.

The World's Bible

Christ has no hands but our hands
To do His work today,
He has no feet but our feet
To lead men in His way.
He has no tongue but our tongues
To tell men how He died.
He has no help but our help
To bring them to His side.

We are the only Bible
The careless world will read.
We are the sinner's Gospel
We are the scoffer's creed.
We are the Lord's last message
Given in deed and word.
What if the type is crooked?
What if the print is blurred?

What if our hands are busy
With other work than His?
What if our feet are walking

Where sin's allurement is?
What if our tongues are speaking
Of things His lips would spurn?
How can we hope to help Him
And hasten His return?

To hasten our Lord's return
We truly need much power,
So let us all be Spirit-filled
And awaiting Him each hour,
In an hour that we think not,
He said He should appear;
Then let us walk in holiness,
And meet Him with a cheer.

As stated in the poem, Herman was convinced he needed to be the hands and feet and shoulders of Christ. If someone's barn burned down, Herman was there to help build it back up; if someone's baby was crying, Herman was there to hold it; if you lost your job, Herman was at your door with an arm-load of groceries. Being a member of the Old Brethren Church, he would easily have been mistaken for Amish in his appearance. But his church group was similar to the German Baptist Church, giving members the freedom to drive cars, use modern appliances and electricity in their homes, and individually determine the value of using computers and other modern technology.

As soon as Herman and Tom met, it was a Paul and Timothy friendship. Together they visited the sick, counseled the mentally ill, and opened a temporary medical clinic in Herman's basement where Herman's wife, Carol, often assisted Tom.

Although Tom became a member of the Old Brethren Church, neither I nor the children did. But we attended services and fellowshipped together. I worried about whether or not I should follow my husband in this endeavor and join the church.

With great wisdom and love, Herman and one of the ministering elders told me that it was not necessary for me to become a member unless I really wanted to. They said they had seen few couples with as much oneness in their marriage as Tom and I had in ours. They explained that love and unity in a marriage is not guaranteed by membership in the same church fellowship. I was grateful for their understanding and observations, and I was thankful that Tom finally had a very solid, genuine church home that accepted him just the way he was.

The practice at the depot in Camden continued to grow. Tom made house calls to shut-ins; he traded services for a supply of wood; he handled emergencies from bee stings to a midwife's call for help while delivering a baby. As he became immersed in the community and culture of the people around us, he realized a need wasn't being met locally. Many people who lost loved ones through old age or sickness were not interested in spending exorbitant sums on burial services. The cost of an expensive casket was a burden and an unnecessary extravagance to these folks. Because of Tom's friendship with Herman, he knew an Amish man in Nappanee who built and sold caskets at a reasonable price. Practical as Tom was, he decided to stock a supply of caskets in the office attic as a courtesy to some of his patients.

One night, we received a call that the wife of a missionary friend had died. Did we have a casket? Well, yes, we did. Even though it was about eleven o'clock at night, we all climbed into our farm truck to go to the office and get a casket. With Tom and the two older kids, we tried to haul the casket out of the attic, down the stairs, and into the truck. Of course, we dropped it on the way to the truck and the kids started blaming each other.

"Hold your end up!"

"I can't. It's too heavy."

"Ssh! Look! The lights just went on in that house. You're waking people up. Everyone in town is going to think we're sneaking a dead body out of the office."

"I can't help it."

"Yes, you can. Now push."

"Quiet! Don't just drop it in the truck bed."

"Well, nobody is in it! What does it matter?"

"Well, maybe somebody doesn't want their casket all banged up!"

"Shove your end forward, and keep quiet. Dead people don't care about their casket!"

Tom and I were laughing so hard we couldn't stand up straight. But we got the casket loaded and delivered to the family in need.

When Tom realized what a burden funeral expenses were to some of his patients, he began working with state senator Katie Wolfe. Together they tried to pass an amendment to the state law that would decrease some of the expensive requirements for funerals. The amendment failed, but he made a lasting friend in Senator Wolfe and continued to inform his patients of less expensive options for caskets.

Tom was always busy. If he wasn't doctoring or supplying caskets, he was making pottery and working on the farm. The farm had become his haven. But it kept us all occupied trying to keep up with the menagerie.

CHAPTER 8

"OLD MACDONALD HAD A FARM"

THE PRACTICE FLOURISHED, AND SO did the farm. We sold our own honey, showed dairy goats at local livestock shows, milked a Jersey cow, raised registered Dorset sheep, managed a small apple orchard, collected sap for maple syrup, and did many other activities on the farm.

The habits of bees had always fascinated Tom. He taught each of the children to wear netted hats, long-sleeved shirts, and white pants banded at the ankles and to carry smokers while harvesting honey from the hives. Framed combs of honey were placed in a galvanized metal extractor that spun the golden liquid out through a pipe at the bottom. Our oldest son held glass jars under the spigot to catch the honey, but he wasn't old enough to worry about his habit of licking the rim of the jar before capping it. We labeled and boxed the honey (that he didn't lick) for sale or gifts.

Loving the science behind genetics, Tom learned how to artificially inseminate our dairy goats so we could improve our breeding stock. We raised Swiss Oberhasli dairy goats for many years, using their milk for drinking and for cheese making. Tom enjoyed making both hard and soft cheese so much that he eventually bought a milk cow. When our youngest daughter was old enough to go to the barn with him, he would sit her on Bessie's back while he milked. Tom saved a gallon of milk for household use and fed the other four gallons to our chickens, turkeys, and two pigs.

Many animals came and went on our farm, but the sheep stayed throughout the years. Until Tom became too busy in his practice, he often helped with the sheep. At lambing time in January, we took turns helping the ewes safely deliver their lambs. Crouched in the warm straw, watching our breath make smoke-like puffs in the frosty air, we would wait patiently for a mother in labor. With the frigid winter temperatures, it was important that each baby was dried off immediately and nursed from the mother.

"Here come the feet," I whispered one cold night as we sat together waiting for a birth. "She seems awfully slow. Do you think we should help her?"

"Not yet. Let's give her a little more time. I hate to pull too soon," Tom said.

I settled back into the straw and hugged myself from the cold. Tom was sitting with his legs stretched out in front of him and his head leaning against the wooden stanchion at his back. The wooly ewe rested on her side and gave a low moan every few minutes as her sides contracted. Dusty cobwebs hung between the rafters of the barn roof. A cat meowed from the corner. Outside the barn window, the gentle dance of snowflakes swirled in moonlight-dusted winter gusts. I shivered and leaned against Tom.

"What do you think is going to happen to us?" I asked, pensively.

"Tonight?" Tom asked.

I punched his arm. "No! I mean the big picture. What do you think is going to happen to the Christian community in this country? Do you think we will be persecuted for our faith one day?"

Tom shrugged. "Probably. But we knew that when we signed up."

I sighed with resignation. "Yeah, you're right. I don't think we thought much about it then, though. We just thought about Jesus and heaven and sharing the gospel."

Tom was quiet for a minute, and then said, "It's about relationships."

"What do you mean?" I pressed. "You're not making sense."

"Everything," Tom replied, "is about relationships. Life. The gospel. Christianity. It's all about relationships. In the end, all we have is our relationship with God and with people, especially our family. If we screw that up, we screw up everything important."

With a loud grunt and a great heave, the ewe's sides tensed and little white legs shot out, up to the knee joints. I leaned forward.

Tom put his hand on my shoulder and held me back. "Let her do her job. Give her a chance to do it on her own."

I sat back on my haunches, rocking slowly on my heels to keep my balance. "So, how do we reconcile our relationship with your parents?"

"That, I don't have an answer for," Tom said. "Sometimes I think it takes a lifetime to reconcile some relationships, and even then there may be gaps that just can't be closed in the time we have on earth. With my parents, I always felt like I was aching for their love and attention and approval. I never felt like I had those things, whether it was because I really didn't have them or because I just *felt* like I didn't, I don't know. I figured maybe I wasn't worth loving; maybe I was just a rotten kid."

The ewe grunted and pushed a little pink nose followed by a slippery, wet head and shoulders through the birth canal. She paused only slightly before giving one more push. The back legs slid out with a gush of blood and afterbirth.

Tom reached over and cleaned the mucus out of the lamb's mouth. There was no cough or reflex to indicate life. A tinge of blue shaded the wet newborn's lips. Tom grabbed the lamb, covered its nostrils, and breathed into the tiny mouth. With a cough and a sputter, the lamb jerked back its head and choked with life. A second pair of feet poked out the birth canal. The twin, slightly smaller, came much faster, gasping for air as soon as it slid onto the straw.

We rubbed both lambs with towels until they were dry and bleating for food. They were strong, healthy babies. In a matter of minutes, they were nuzzling the mother and loudly sucking their first warm milk. Tom adjusted a heat lamp safely above the straw and threw the damp towel over his arm. I carried my towel and followed him. As we stepped from the shelter of the barn door into the swirling snow, I grasped Tom's arm and recited a poem that my father had often recited to me:

> They strolled down the lane together,
> The sky was studded with stars.
> They reached the gate in silence.
> He lifted down the bars.
> She neither smiled nor thanked him
> Because she knew not how
> For he was just a farmer's boy
> And she was a Jersey cow.

Tom smiled as we reached the house. Tossing our towels on the laundry-room floor, we kicked off our barn boots and hung up our jackets.

Reaching for Tom's hand, I said, "Tom, any parent should be so proud of you. You are worth loving."

Smiling wistfully, he shrugged. "Let's go to bed. I'm tired."

Our sheep flock grew. We ate lamb meat and sold meat to individual buyers as well as the local sale barn. Even when our children left for college and married, we continued the sheep business. One day, when our oldest son was a college senior and our youngest son was a high-school freshman, we asked the boys to take a lamb to the butchering plant in a near-by town. It was spring break for the boys, so we were glad to have the extra help around the farm.

The boys tied the seventy-pound lamb's legs together and put it in the back of the truck. It was about a ten-mile trip to town. The morning hours passed without any truck returning from the processing plant. I began to worry but decided the boys probably stopped somewhere along the way. Still, a mother's worst fears nagged at the edge of my thoughts as I washed dishes. Finally, I heard the truck rumbling up the drive. The back door slammed, and I heard barn boots stomping their way down the hall while irritated voices rose.

"It's all your fault!"

"No, it isn't. You should have helped more."

"What do you mean? I couldn't back the truck up and unload too."

"You should have gotten off your butt and out of the truck."

"You should have moved faster. Besides, what kind of an idiot holds a lamb between his legs?"

"I wouldn't have tried to hold it if you had tied the legs tighter. It's your fault!"

"Boys," I interrupted, "where is the lamb?"

"We lost it, and it's his fault," said our college boy, with a nod toward his brother.

"It's not my fault!" screamed our high-school boy, throwing up his hands.

"You lost our lamb?" I asked, exasperated.

"I didn't lose it," insisted our college boy. "*He* lost it. We tried to catch it but it ran all over town, through people's flower beds and yards. So we called animal control."

I was torn between rolling on the floor in hysterical laughter and scolding the boys for leaving a lamb to run through other people's property. The back door slammed again as our married daughter came walking down the hallway. The story was retold with heated accusations and insults.

With hands on hips, she exclaimed incredulously, "So, dumb and dumber lost a lamb in town!"

This set off another round of excuses and finger-pointing.

For the rest of the afternoon, I waited on a phone call saying that animal control had captured a lamb. No call came. I invited my daughter and son-in-law for supper. Tom came home, and the family chattered around the table like noisy chipmunks.

"Guess what!" exclaimed our son-in-law, who dispatched at the local sheriff's office during the day while taking college classes at night. "We had the most hilarious call today. Somebody lost a lamb in town. It was running all over the place. We put a notice out that there was a lamb on the lam."

"He did it!" declared our college boy, defensively.

"I did not! It was your fault!" insisted our high-school boy.

"It was Dumb and Dumber," our daughter added.

Tom and our youngest daughter stared around the table, putting the pieces of the story together.

"Wait a minute," said our son-in-law, with his eyes as big as saucers. "That wasn't *your* lamb was it?"

"He should have tied the legs tighter," repeated our college boy.

"I did tie them!" protested our high-school boy. "You should have gotten out of the truck instead of just sitting there and making me do all the work."

Our son-in-law was laughing so hard he dropped to the floor.

Tom and I gathered the dishes from the table and carried them to the sink. We stood together, looking out the window above the sink. Fields of growing crops, pastures with quietly grazing sheep, chickens scratching in the dirt, and cotton-ball clouds in a blue sky were framed by the window casing.

Tom chuckled, "We have a good life, you know."

"Some days," I said, laughing, and glancing toward the table where the boys were still arguing. "We have a great life!"

Although it involved a lot of work, life on the farm was truly very good. In February and March, Tom tapped the maple trees and sent the boys out to gather the buckets of sap. In one of the small out buildings, Tom built a system where we could boil the sap down to syrup. It took a matter of days and about fifty gallons of sap to make a quart of golden, sweet syrup.

There seemed to be work for every season, but summers were always the busiest. Tom's green thumb produced a bountiful vegetable garden as well as a productive orchard and stunning flower gardens. Eventually, Tom had a brick wall built to provide privacy for what we all called his "secret garden." He dug a pond, surrounded it with rose bushes, stocked it with koi, and laid the edges of the pond with fossil rocks from the creek. He poured a cement patio and had the boys help him build a grape arbor over it.

Besides being a beautiful haven, where clematis and roses flourished, it was a favorite family spot for parties, Bible studies, and morning coffee. Tom and I often enjoyed the garden while sipping coffee and listening to mourning doves coo in the pine trees while wind chimes sang their musical notes in a gentle breeze.

"Don't you ever get tired?" I asked Tom one morning as we drank coffee on the patio.

"Yeah, but there's so much I want to do!" he exclaimed.

"What more could you possibly want?"

"Well, I would still like to build a cabin. And I haven't developed my pottery to the level I want to reach yet. I have some very nice pieces, but there is so much more I want to experiment with in colors and glazes."

With the children, Tom and I bought and tore down a ten-by-twelve-foot kiln and rebuilt it on the farm. By the time we were finished, we were as black as the soot that covered the kiln bricks. With their dad, the children learned to make clay pots on a pottery wheel in our basement and fire them in the kiln. One of the most beautiful glazes Tom learned to use was a crystalline glaze of light-green on aqua. His vases with this glaze looked like the wind blew the leaves of a gingko tree against the damp clay and left their fan-shaped form behind. Tom made cups, spoon holders, vases, a few plates, and one little bear with a basket in his arms for toothpicks.

Tom's tremendous creative energy and skills were expressed through harvesting honey, artificially inseminating goats, designing and maintaining a pond, landscaping with roses, reaping produce from the land and trees, and designing pottery. Most people admired or even envied his ability to develop so many skills and to participate actively in so many hobbies.

For many years, we thought Tom was extremely gifted, and he was. But his high levels of energy, his skillfulness, and his creative mind racing from one interest to the next were indicative of something deeper. Regardless of the source, Tom's hobbies kept our farm a busy place. The office flourished, the farm was thriving, and our house itself became a beehive of activity.

CHAPTER 9

A HOUSE LIKE ELVIS'S

OUR HOME WAS A HUB of non-stop activity. It was not uncommon to have a patient sleeping in one room or another. For several weeks, we had a man from the horse-and-buggy community in a hospital bed in our living room. His horse had run over him while pulling a cart loaded with wood. A member of our family was often called upon to give up his or her bedroom to a patient with a medical emergency. As Herman observed our living situation and lack of family and patient privacy, he emphatically stated that we needed an addition of some type on our house. We agreed.

Tom designed an addition that allowed two bedrooms, a bath, and a kitchenette for patients, plus extra bedrooms and a living room for our family. This project was a labor of love built by the Old Brethren Church members from Nappanee, along with many local people. Once a week, for a year, thirty or forty men and boys came rolling up the drive in their trucks and vans, armed with hammers, saws, drills, and everything else needed for the construction of the addition. I cooked dinner for them while they framed, ran plumbing, put on roofing and siding, and laid flooring. Like clockwork, about the same time every afternoon, tools would be returned to boxes, hats and coats would be gathered, and the brethren would depart for home, where many of them operated dairies with cows waiting to be milked.

As the addition began to take place, we realized what a large home we had designed. One of the kids walked through the house and counted the new rooms plus the existing ones. "Wow! We now have twenty-three rooms, just like the Elvis Presley house at Graceland."

Tom and I prayed that God would use the space for His purpose. He did use our house in many different ways of ministry. As we continued to teach our children at home over the years, we became active in a local group of home-schooling families. For these families and their children, we hosted teen parties, father-daughter dinners, dances, and slumber parties. Eventually, we even hosted some college dinners when our "kids" went to Purdue University.

One Sunday every month, the brethren from Nappanee had church in our garage. After the service, everyone set up tables, and we had lunch together. There were usually about a hundred people. Some local people always joined us, and it was a great day of worship, fellowship, and friendship.

We also treated many patients in our home. There were times when an insurance company allowed only a certain number of days in the hospital for a specific illness or procedure. On several occasions, we cared for patients who should have been allowed more time in the hospital but were dismissed early for insurance reasons. There were other people who had no insurance or who did not want to go to the hospital. One elderly man, who was dying, did not want to die in the hospital. Tom brought him to our house, where he died peacefully in one of the new patient rooms with Tom at his side.

We delivered nine babies and treated pneumonia, kidney stones, mastitis, severe depression, and other maladies in the back part of our house. There were always those times when something would happen that reminded us how homespun our operation was. After delivering one of the babies, I was mopping the floor of the "delivery room" when Tom called me into the hallway.

"I can't catch the dog," he whispered urgently.

"What do you mean, you can't catch the dog? Why are you messing with the dog?" I whispered back, tired from the long labor and delivery and from mopping blood off the floor.

"It has the placenta!" he confessed.

"What?" I hissed.

"The dog has the placenta."

"How did the dog get the placenta?" I glared at him.

"Well," he said, sheepishly, "I took everything out to the trash. I was going to burn it, but I forgot the matches. Before I got back to the house, one of the dogs went running by with the placenta swinging from his mouth."

I leaned against the wall and covered my face. "Good grief! The relatives are coming to see the new baby."

For one tired minute, we looked at each other. "We'll get the kids," we said together.

Calling our oldest ones, we explained that one of the dogs had the placenta from the recent delivery and someone needed to catch him and burn the afterbirth before the family arrived to see the baby. They stared at us, horrified. Plenty of times they had seen the afterbirth from a sheep or goat, but a human placenta being drug around the yard took the birth experience to a whole different level.

"I'm going to finish mopping," I declared as I turned my back and took my stand against being any part of the fiasco.

"Hurry up," Tom urged the kids into motion.

To this day, I don't know the details or who did the dirty work. I just know that the matter was taken care of. At future births, Tom was much more careful with the clean-up. "And how about the placenta?" became something of a family joke.

After we built the addition, we moved our casket supply from the office to the house, where there was now a large walk-in attic. The caskets were one of the favorite spots for hide-and-seek, which was played frequently over the years.

The basement was Tom's haven. In the expansive basement, he had his pottery wheel, his clay, and his chemicals - plus his own private bathroom, where no one could bother him. When Tom was under stress or experiencing depression, he often sat at the potter's wheel and turned mugs or bowls. As long as he was busy caring for people, his mind didn't wander to the dark places that haunted him. Many times, we sat and talked in the basement as Tom molded the clay.

"You've been depressed, haven't you?" I asked, watching his hands shape a coffee mug.

"Underneath it all, I always feel depressed," he admitted.

"Is there anything I can do to help?"

"You always help. You and the kids are the only reason I keep going. The older I get, the worse it is. I watch my own children grow, and I realize things that were absent from my early years. When did I laugh? When was I innocent? When was I a child without worry, fear, and shame? I don't remember anything like that. Where are my memories? What happened to my childhood? Did I have one?"

"Oh, Tom," I said, sadly, sliding my arms around his neck. "I don't have any answers. But look at what you have given your own children. They have known such love and laughter and protection. You have given all of us so much."

Tom laughed. "At least they got to have any animal they wanted."

And that they did. Besides patients and parties and family events, the house always had an assortment of animals. One night in bed, I felt something move by my feet.

"Tom, wake up!" I said, in alarm.

"What's wrong?" he asked, groggily turning the light on.

I jumped out of bed. "There's something under the covers. It's crawling up beside you!"

Tom jumped from the bed and threw the blankets back. Our oldest son's ferret darted under the pillow. If it wasn't a ferret, it was something else. Our daughter had been persuaded that a rabbit could be litter-trained and kept in the house. We yelled at her every time we found rabbit poop in the cracks of the sofa cushions. She also kept a baby raccoon for several months that was frequently found darting from room to room. But it wasn't always the kids. During one freezing day in January, there were half-frozen lambs snuggling in front of the woodstove, a baby calf warming in the bathtub, and peeping chicks under a heat lamp in the kitchen. To be truthful, this was a pretty routine occurrence every January.

Tom added to the menagerie when he decided to raise registered toy poodles. The first one he bought he named Bill. Mr. Bill went to the office and the nursing home, and he made house calls with Tom. Twice a year, one of the female poodles was delivering puppies somewhere in the house.

Even the llama we kept to guard our sheep got his day in the house. We had a birthday party and invited our neighbor Ethel. Ethel was a saint who adopted us the day we moved in. She helped preserve the endless supply of garden produce; she helped with the children, the laundry, the dishes - anything else she could put her hands on. As she grew older, it was difficult for her to walk. When Ethel declared at the birthday party that she had never seen a llama, our son-in-law decided she needed to see one up close. The llama was brought through the back door and down the hallway, clicking his heels right into the living room. Ethel was delighted.

When Ethel passed away, we provided the casket and held the funeral service at our house. She would have loved it.

Tom enjoyed entertaining in our home. Fortunately, I did too. For several years, we hosted a dinner for the community and invited singing groups to provide music. Between 350 and 500 people, came for the food, fellowship, and fun. Tom and I provided a main dish and drinks while everyone else brought something to contribute.

One year, Tom wanted to serve navy-bean soup with ham and cornbread. He had purchased a huge cast-iron pot just for the occasion. Never having cooked such a large quantity of navy beans before, I wasn't sure if the pot was a good idea. Tom's idea was to let the soup simmer for several days to "blend the flavors." Around 9:00 a.m. on the day of the picnic, we sampled the simmering soup. It was rancid! It had spoiled at the low temperature.

Tom sent one of boys after more ham, and I flew to the store to buy twenty-five pounds of beans. I reminded the Lord that He could feed five thousand on two loaves of bread and five fish. "Today," I pleaded, "You only have to make bean soup for five hundred."

He did. Never have I heard so many people compliment navy-bean soup as that day. Repeatedly, we were told it was the best bean soup they had ever tasted. Tom and I would look at each other and just smile.

The year our daughter was married, we stopped having the community picnic. It would have conflicted with the wedding that year. But Tom and I were ready to slow down a little bit anyway.

If it wasn't a patient or a friend or a relative, there was always someone extra staying at the house. When Tom learned about an elderly physician from Afghanistan, who was driving from Indianapolis to Logansport (about a ninety-mile trip) for his job, Tom immediately offered him a room in our basement. When the World Trade Center went down and relations with the Middle East became strained, our resident physician started making regular phone calls to his family back home. Tom and I would ask each other every morning if this would be the day we would get up and find our house surrounded by FBI or CIA agents.

As the years passed, everyone was growing older, especially our children. When they began to go to college, marry, and leave home, Tom and I recognized a new purpose for our big house. Many of Tom's elderly patients were developing some form of dementia. One spouse would be caring for the failing one. Preparing a meal was a daunting task for these couples, and socializing was even more difficult. We decided to open a once-a-month restaurant in our home. Tom and I cooked, and our two younger children who were still home helped serve and clean up. We named the restaurant The Fritz after our son's favorite cat, which, of course, lived in the house (but we kept him shut up, because it would have been illegal to have a cat running around a restaurant ... uh huh).

It quickly became too big a chore for us, but friends gladly volunteered to help serve the dinner. We charged three dollars for the meal, knowing that we were serving a generation that would not feel comfortable unless they paid their own way. It was great fun, and the older people so appreciated the food and the opportunity to visit. Tom bought a chef's hat, which he donned with his apron as he cooked and visited with everyone who came. He loved to tease and joke with each one.

Because people were always coming and going, we never locked the doors to our house. On one occasion, this proved to be a bit awkward. The kids and I came home to find Tom laughing on the couch.

"What are you laughing at?" I asked with a smile, knowing it must be funny.

"I got caught," he chuckled, half gasping for air.

Since he was stretched out in his boxer shorts, I figured someone caught him in his underwear. "So, what happened?" I asked again.

He was turning red, his legs were flailing, and he could hardly talk from laughing so hard.

"Come on," I insisted, "I want to hear about it."

As he gasped for air, he explained. "I had just gotten out of the shower when I heard voices. There were some folks here looking for me, but I only had my boxers on. I hid behind the door while they walked by. Then I ran out the back door behind them and came in the side porch. They were walking through the house, calling out to see if anyone was home. I kept sneaking around from room to room, just out of their sight. They finally gave up, and I watched from the upstairs window until they left. It was hilarious!"

A lot of people came looking for Tom. Besides local people, many came from far away for medical care, advice, and fellowship. Howard came from Alberta, Canada; Willard and Thelma came from Pennsylvania; Elmo came from a plain community in Tennessee. Dr. and Mrs. Chang came from Indianapolis and brought friends from their Chinese Bible study. They brought Chinese food in exchange for horseback rides and a farm tour.

In spite of the many people that came to our home, it was still a place of refuge for Tom. He loved his vegetable garden and his rose garden. He loved the little balcony outside our bedroom where he could watch thunderstorms roll in and lightning flash above the fields. People came for help, and if Tom could help them, he did. It was his own wounded soul that he was never able to heal.

CHAPTER 10

MY FAVORITE CASHEW

ALTHOUGH OUR LIFE WAS OFTEN filled with laughter, there were times we didn't laugh. There were times when I could see Tom's emotional stability beginning to fray at the edges, and my heart ached.

As the years passed, Tom's inability to sleep became an increasing problem. He tried a glass of wine at night, but the need for more and more alcohol soon became a concern. Worried about his growing dependency, he joined Alcoholics Anonymous. After his first meeting, I asked if he thought the group would help him.

"Yeah, I think it will help a lot. I met four other doctors there that I know," he said.

There were other behaviors that were manifesting more clearly with age. Tom had always exhibited a much higher than average energy level. With age, it was becoming easier to identify these periods of excessive energy as part of the mood swings from mania to depression and back again. One Sunday afternoon, he disappeared without telling any of us where he was going. Finally, in the late afternoon, he called to say that he had purchased a swimming pool for the family. When I asked where he was, he proudly declared that he had driven to Indianapolis, an hour and a half away, and purchased the half-price pool.

Another weekend, he returned home after a long absence and excitedly told us that he had decided to visit the Pentecostal Church. "They were singing hymns," he said with exuberance, "and I decided to get right up on stage and lead the singing. Everyone loved it!"

Cringing, I told him gently, "Tom, you need some medication."

"No, I feel great. I feel better than I have for a long time. You just don't want me to be happy. I feel so good! I feel like the sexiest man alive." He grinned.

During the times he felt good, he would often watch television late at night and purchase items offered during commercials. Surprise boxes would come to the house: a special pair of gloves to wear when peeling potatoes, a new type of food processor (one for each of our married children, too), an electric machine to wash eyeglasses. Some of the boxes sat in our basement unopened.

As a family, we had suspected that Tom was experiencing symptoms of manic-depressive disorder, but convincing him to get treatment was not easy. Finally, he talked to a psychiatrist friend who said he was exhibiting classic, textbook symptoms of the illness. Later that night, Tom lay in bed with his hands on his forehead in agony.

"You're married to a nut. I'm so sorry. I shouldn't have married you. I'm crazy. How does it feel to be married to a nut?" he asked with pain and humiliation evident in his voice.

I had been lying on my back beside him. I rolled over on my side and pressed two fingers to his lips. "Stop, Tom. If you're a nut, then you're my favorite cashew."

Tom reached up and took my hand. "I love you from the bottom of my heart."

"I know," I said, smiling through the tears. "I know."

We approached two psychiatrists and one medical doctor in our attempts to find help. One psychiatrist suggested Tom should never have gotten married with the childhood abuse he had endured. Another suggested that Tom drop his Judeo-Christian beliefs and re-evaluate his childhood experiences from a positive perspective. The physician we saw walked into the room, sat down at his desk, and started clipping his fingernails as he told us about his personal life and counseled Tom to read passages in the Bible to deal with his illness and his childhood memories. As a result, we gave up looking for outside help. On our own, we asked God for guidance, searched the Scriptures, and combed the bookstore shelves for literature that might help us.

Authors that helped us both were M. Scott Peck, MD: Susan Forward, PhD; and Stephen D. Grubman-Black, PhD. Peck helped us understand how much a person's childhood can be affected by the parenting they receive. Even with all our cultural progress in America, we fail to grasp the simple truth expressed in Proverbs 22:6: "Train up a child in the way he should go; and when he is old, he will not depart from it." The reason a child will not depart from his early training is because he can't. Those early years establish a foundation in the psyche of a developing human that is difficult, if not impossible, to alter.

From Forward, we learned that, in the same household, each sibling might experience and react to his or her childhood differently. Tom had felt isolated for so long in his memories, or lack thereof, compared to those of his siblings. While reading Forward's book, he realized that his siblings simply could not identify with him because their experiences and personalities were different from his.

Through Grubman-Black, Tom identified much of his unspoken conflict, confusion, and pain as he read the author's personal experience of dealing with childhood molestation. But no amount of reading, praying, or talking could make Tom well. The medication helped, but his manic-depressive disorder was worsening with age. And his personal reflections of childhood experiences caused him increasing anguish as the years passed.

When Tom wasn't excessively happy, boisterous, and spending money, he was severely depressed. There were days when he simply said, "Make sure the guns are locked up."

I would sit beside him and ask, "Do you want to talk about it?"

"Something happens inside the brain," he would say, "when children are violated. When a child is growing and developing, there are so many foundations being laid for the future. God didn't design us to handle abuse. Even my concept of God as a loving Father has been tainted. I have never been able to see myself as a person whom God loves and cherishes. I must be one of those vessels God made for destruction."

"Tom, that's not true," I insisted. "Look, God found you. He rescued you. He gave the children and me to you. He has blessed our life in so many incredible ways."

"It just seems like no matter how hard I work or how fast I run, I can never outrun what happened to me as a child," he said sadly.

"I know," I sighed, "but you are so much more than that little boy who was abused."

"Am I?" he asked. "Every day I wake up, I see that little boy longing for love and attention. Then I remember that man making me feel dirty and ashamed and threatening me. He said if I told anyone, the sheriff would put me in jail. I believed him."

"Tom, you were a child. What he did to you was wrong and evil. You believed him because that's what children do; they trust adults. Adults should be worthy of such trust."

Tom looked at me with a pained expression. "Why? Why did God let it happen?"

"Oh, Tom, I don't know the why. I do know that this is planet earth, not the Garden of Eden. There is something in our hearts that longs for the rightness of Eden; but it isn't here. Earth is where men get to make choices, and so many of those choices are selfish, evil, and devastating to others." I hung my head, filled with sorrow for the pain I knew Tom was experiencing.

"You know," Tom confessed, "I took the drugs in high school because I hated myself. I thought it was all my fault. I wanted to kill myself. And yet something in me wanted to live. I wanted to start all over and be normal and happy and clean."

"I know," I said.

"Why didn't my parents get help for me?"

"Tom, I don't know. Maybe they didn't know how to help you. Maybe they didn't understand what it was doing to you on the inside. I'm sure everyone reacts differently to trauma. Maybe they thought you could overcome it on your own. It's probably a lot more complicated than you or I will ever figure out in this life."

Although it was hard to justify the pain, it was this deep, emotional grief that enabled Tom to have so much humility, understanding, and compassion. At his office, he kept an unsigned poem that reflected his heart.

Bit of Advice

Pray don't find fault
With the man who limps,
Or stumbles along the road,
Unless you have worn the shoes he wears,
Or struggled beneath his load.

There may be tacks
In his shoes that hurt
Though hidden from view.
Or the burden he bears
Placed on your back
Might cause you to stumble, too.

Don't sneer at the man

Who's down today,
Unless you have felt the blow
That caused his fall
Or felt his shame
That only the fallen know.
You may be strong,
But still the blows,
That were his
If dealt to you
In the selfsame way
At the selfsame time
Might cause you to stagger, too.

Don't be too harsh with
The man who sins,
Or pelt him with words
Or stones,
Unless you are sure, yea
Doubly sure
That you have no sins
Of your own.

For you know perhaps,
If the tempter's voice
Should whisper as soft
To you,
As it did to him when he
Went astray
T'would cause you
To falter, too.

It was Tom's personal pain and struggles that made him
so gentle and kind with others. But, still, the mental disorder

worsened and threatened to take over more of Tom's personality and behavior.

Professionally, he was always one to try innovative methods of healing or treatment. His open-mindedness and his manic-depressive state often made him susceptible to impractical purchases for the office. One of those purchases was a medical laser. We knew that his decision was partially based on the euphoria of a manic episode, but it also reflected his desire to make people feel good about their appearance.

The laser was a 130,000 dollar purchase that eliminated acne scars, age spots, unwanted hair, leg veins, and other skin blemishes. Because of the laser, Tom also purchased a line of scientifically advanced skin-care products. He was very excited about his new venture; I was skeptical. Having state-of-the-art technology in Camden meant we offered big-city treatments at small-town prices. But men and women came from Lafayette and other surrounding cities. A couple of women flew from Florida because the prices were so good. Tom loved it when someone walked out of the office feeling better about his or her appearance.

Poor financial decisions, excessive buying, inflated perceptions of self, and inappropriate conversation are all part of being manic-depressive, but God always seemed to be one step ahead of us, protecting us from disaster. And people loved Doc Anderson so much that, if he got a little out of hand, well, they loved him anyway.

As the practice grew and Tom moved from the depot to a large bank building across the street, in God's great scheme of things, He brought Linda to assist Tom at the office. She was hand-picked for service. Her heart, like Tom's, was to serve Christ through serving people, and she also kept the doctor in line. When Tom bought a surplus of goldfish and decided to have aquariums in the office, Linda did the maintenance. When the office basement started bulging at the seams with Tom's reserve supplies, Linda hauled them out when he was gone. Most of all, she kept a close eye on Tom.

Two events that worsened Tom's condition were the marriages of his oldest two children and a division in the Old Brethren Church. As the children left home, he felt abandoned. Never believing he was worth loving anyway, he took their steps of independence personally. One of the first things he did after our oldest daughter married was buy a pet Snugli and a new puppy. He carried the pup around the house on his tummy the way he had carried his little girl. Losing his son to a beautiful, young art student at Purdue was just as devastating. His psyche didn't know how to process these experiences in a positive way. He interpreted the marriages as loss, rejection, and abandonment.

Tom had been a member of the Old Brethren Church for ten years when an internal disagreement caused it to divide. Tom could not and would not choose sides. He loved the brethren dearly. Once again, he lost his source of fellowship. The Old Brethren community had provided so much stability for him spiritually as well as emotionally.

The impact of his children's marriages and the loss of his church fellowship, added to the normal process of aging, began to eat away at his equilibrium. I watched him falter and begin to lose direction. It was like watching someone who couldn't see the road clearly anymore try to shake his head, clear his eyes, and keep running in spite of blurred images clouding his vision and demons breathing over his shoulder.

However, there was one very bright spot that never failed to bring laughter, relief, and good memories: our family vacations.

CHAPTER 11

THE WRONG SIDE
OF LAKE LOUISE

BECAUSE TOM WAS EASILY ACCESSIBLE to the community, it became important for us to leave town occasionally for a vacation. For one reason or another, our vacations never seemed ordinary. In the early years, we went north to Wisconsin. One day, just north of Milwaukee, we decided to hike the sandy beach on the west side of Lake Michigan. The day was hot, and the water was cool. With toddlers in tow, Tom and I wandered into the water, letting the waves lap against our legs. The children splashed and tried to catch the whitecaps. A fly landed on my arm, then another. Suddenly, Tom and I both cried out as a cloud of biting, black flies descended over us and the children. Yelling and swatting, we ran toward the car, which was about a quarter of a mile away. Out of breath, we jumped into the car and slammed the doors.

"Wow!" Tom said, "That was bizarre!"

"No kidding," I agreed. "That was kind of like a nightmare from the *Twilight Zone.*

"Mommy," asked our son, "do we have to go to the beach anymore?"

"Not today," Tom and I said together.

Vacations were special times for Tom to be with his family. He took the boys to the Minnesota Boundary Waters for a "rite of passage" camping trip. We walked through the Biltmore estate, talked beside quiet streams in the Smoky Mountains, gathered shells along the coast of Maine, played in the sand on Anna Marie Island, hiked the caverns at Carlsbad, and ate chowder in Nova Scotia. One bright morning, we chased each other down the white sands of the Tularosa Basin in New Mexico as the sun came up. We watched the geysers erupt at Yosemite, shopped Indian pueblos in Taos, and walked curiously around the Devil's Tower in Colorado.

Showing his family God's creation was Tom's way of saying, "That's all His. From the Grand Canyon to the gardens of Vancouver are displays of His awesome majesty, power, and diversity."

We loved the canyons and the desert. For a couple of years, we owned a small home in Benson, Arizona. Because a couple of families that we knew also owned homes in Benson, we always had friends to do things with when we vacationed there. With one of these friends, we went rattlesnake hunting. We drove through the desert until we came to an underground cave, and Tom, the boys, and our friend went into the cave with a snare at the end of a long pole. Being the winter months, the snakes moved more slowly than in the summer. The girls and I stayed outside the cave and prayed. Inside the cave, the boys directed the beam of their flashlights against the walls and ledges until they located beady eyes and slight movement. Then the snares flew. There was something very "man triumphs over beast" about coming out of the cave, hands clasped just behind a snake's venomous head, and six feet of a slithering rattler dangling in the air. Local restaurants gladly bought the snakes and offered rattlesnake meat on their menus.

Tom also liked to hunt the wild pigs that roamed the mesquite-dotted desert. Called javelina, these pigs were a lot smaller than domestic farm pigs. Thankfully, the meat tasted mostly like the barbecue sauce it was often cooked in.

Of course, Tom and our two oldest children had to hike to the bottom of the Grand Canyon at least once. I stayed at the top with our second son, who was still a baby. The canyon far surpassed any pictures or descriptions written about it. Vast and incomparable as it was, it stood in second place as our favorite vacation site.

Our favorite trip was to catch the Amtrak train in Chicago and head west until we reached Shelby, Montana. There we rented a car and drove north through the flat plains of southern Alberta and into the breathtaking Canadian Rockies. The first time we made the trip, we rode coach on the train.

Riding coach meant taking whatever seat you could grab on a first-come, first-served basis. Tom and I got our family settled and watched another couple with two children head our direction. The youngsters, about nine and eleven, settled behind Tom and I, while the parents took seats behind their children. As we left Chicago and traveled west into the cattle country of the northern states, childish voices rose to an excited pitch behind us.

"Look, Addie, there's brown cows. Just look at that!" exclaimed the boy.

"I see them! Wow! They're huge!" she squealed, bug-eyed, at the window.

"Those brown cows, Addie, that's where the chocolate milk comes from," said the older and wiser big brother.

"From those cows right there?" She pressed her face against the glass.

"Yep! It's those brown ones right there that make chocolate."

Tom and I looked at each other and shook our heads, both of us thinking, *City kids!* Then the chatter pushed Tom over the edge.

"Hey, Mom!"

"What?" snarled a grouch from the rear.

"Addie's farting!" he bellowed for the entire car to hear.

"Am not!" insisted Addie defensively.

"Yes, you are, and it really smells!" declared favorite brother.

Tom leaned over and stated firmly in my ear, "Last time we ride coach."

And it was. In the following years, we paid the extra money for a private sleeper cabin, where our family got to be together without interruptions.

We rented our car in Shelby and drove toward the Canadian border. After the first trip, it was unanimously decided that someone besides Mom needed to be behind the wheel at the border check. I nervously rolled the window down and declared, "We don't have any drugs," which was followed by a thorough search of our luggage and a thirty-minute delay.

Once we reached the mountains, we would rent a cabin or a motel room and hike the trails to the beautiful, blue-green lakes. One time, as we gathered around Lake Louise, we decided to hike to the opposite end. However, unlike the tourists who were trekking the flat, paved trail to the right of the lake, Tom discovered what looked like a long-lost path through the brush on the opposite side.

"I don't think that's a real trail," I said cautiously.

"Let's try it. We don't want to take that path crowded with tourists. Everybody goes that way. This looks a lot more interesting," Tom insisted as he pushed brush aside and walked ahead.

We pushed back branches and followed in single file - Tom with our youngest daughter on his shoulders, the two boys, our oldest daughter, and me bringing up the rear. The path wound upward, farther and farther above the lake, and the mountain shale became loose and treacherous beneath our feet. The path that had been flat at the beginning became steep and slanted the farther along we went. We needed our hands to steady us, and eventually we needed each other's hands to keep from sliding down the side of the mountain into the ice-cold lake below. As we groped our way along, our chattering stilled, and we listened nervously to crumbling pieces of shale rolling down the mountain and disappearing with a plink into the lake.

"It's just a little farther," Tom said.

"Have you noticed the people on the other side of the lake, Tom?" I asked.

He stopped and looked, then chuckled. "That's funny. They're taking our picture. Some of them are just standing and pointing at us. They're just jealous because their path is boring."

"No," I said, "I think they are probably wondering if they should call for help or if we are total idiots. Maybe they're waiting until one of us rolls into the lake."

Once the path leveled out, we didn't want to go back over it, but we weren't sure about going forward. Tom pressed on.

"It's a lot flatter up here. Just keep coming. I don't think there's a path here, though," he said.

"Really?" I asked with more than a hint of sarcasm.

No, there wasn't a path; we had to make our own. As we got closer to the far end of the lake, the ground became a bog beneath our feet. The bog turned into multiple, ice-cold mountain streams that blocked our path. We jumped over a few of them until we finally came to one too big and too deep to jump. We could either turn back or jump in and wade to the other side. Coming down from the mountain, the water picked up speed as it melted from the glacial ice and swept toward the lake. It was hard to estimate the depth. Since nobody wanted to turn back, Tom handed our daughter to our oldest son and slid into the water. He gasped as it swirled around his waist. "Okay," he said, "slide in and hang onto each other tightly. Nobody let go. We'll make a chain to the other side."

One by one, we held our breath and plunged into the water. Quickly, we scrambled out on the other side, dripping and chilled, but safe. It was a short walk through more boggy ground to reach the paved trail that curved to the far end of the lake. Not many tourists had walked as far as the distant shore, so there was no one there to celebrate our triumphant arrival. However, we were laughing hard and squishing water out of our shoes.

Walking back on the paved side of the lake, I thought of Robert Frost's poem "The Road Less Traveled." In so many ways, Tom walked and led me and our children down a road less traveled. And, as in Frost's poem, it has made a difference in the people we have become, and we are better for it.

CHAPTER 12

THE CAMDEN OFFICE

"DID I TELL YOU ABOUT the one where Mr. Fox caught Mr. Rabbit and Mr. Rabbit says, 'You gonna eat me whole?' Mr. Fox says, 'Nah, I'm gonna spit that part out!'"

Or there was the letter from a Kentucky mother to her son:

Dear Son,

Just a few lines to let you know I'm alive. I'm writing this letter slowly 'cause I know you can't read very fast. You won't know the house when you come, because we moved. I won't be able to send you the address, as the last Kentucky family that lived here took the numbers off for their next house so they won't have to change their address.

About your father, he has a new job. He has over five hundred men under him. He's cutting the grass at the cemetery.

There was a washing machine in the new house when we moved in, but it isn't working too good. Last week, I put fourteen shirts in it, pulled the chain, and I haven't seen them since.

Your sister, Mary, had a baby this morning. I haven't found out if it's a boy or a girl, so I don't know if you're an aunt or an uncle.

Your Uncle Dick drowned last week in the distillery. Some of the workers dove in to save him, but he fought them off bravely. He had his body cremated, and it took three days to put out the fire.

Your father didn't have too much to drink this Christmas. I put a bottle of castor oil in a pint of beer. It kept him going until New Year's Day.

I went to the doctor on Thursday and your father came with me. The doc put a small tube in my mouth and told me not to open it for ten minutes. Your father offered to buy it from him.

It only rained twice last week - three days the first time and four the next.

Monday was so windy that one of our chickens laid the same egg four times.

We got a letter from the undertaker yesterday - he said that if the last statement isn't paid on your grandmother's funeral within seven days, up she comes.

Love, Mother

P.S. I was going to send you ten dollars, but I had already sealed the envelope."

It was the Camden office. Doc Anderson was bouncing from room to room, stethoscope around his neck, telling his favorite jokes or reading his favorite "Letter from a Kentucky mother" that someone had sent him. There was coffee in the waiting room, a little red poodle following Doc, and Linda trying to keep a semblance of order and professionalism.

Jean was often at the front desk. She had been with Tom since the Clymers office. She was one of those efficient, loyal employees that stayed through the moves and changes. Charlene had blessed the office with her talents and hard work until she moved. Donna faithfully ran the billing department. Others came and went, but Linda became the mainstay.

As our children at home required less teaching and attention, I became the office manager who came in on Fridays and other days when necessary. Tom loved to call me to the back office, give me a quick kiss, then run out and tell everyone he was having an affair with the office manager.

Even the drug reps who brought their products to the office liked to visit the practice in Camden. They commented on the office staff camaraderie, the big-hearted doctor, and the obvious concern for the well-being of the patients.

Most of all, the patients knew they were going to be cared for. One patient said it this way:

> A visit was really a visit. You were glad to see him and began feeling better right away. He was on your case. A square, solid man with his beard, suspenders, and distinctive (you might say) haircut, he wasn't the stereotype of a gentle country doctor. He was independent, straight-forward, a fighter, and you'd be surprised how thorough he could be. He'd made the right choice of [his] professional calling. He loved people, loved his life, his large thriving family. He sang in the church choir, raised vegetables, bred dogs,

kept bees, and in his spare time, he worked with clay and wood.

It goes without saying that he made house calls. ... A man like Dr. Anderson raises the quotient of goodness and well-being around him.

I went to a surgical supply store to get a sort of brace he'd prescribed for my (slightly) chipped elbow. There happened to be a power outage, so my credit card was of no use. The proprietor told me to take the brace and pay for it later.

"But you don't even know me," I said. "I've never been here before."

"Oh, that's okay," he said. "You're one of Dr. Tom's."

Tom's genuine concern for his patients sometimes enriched his own medical repertoire of experiences. When a patient with prostate cancer came to him, Tom listened attentively to the man's description of a clinic in southern California that offered alternative cancer treatments. Not wanting to recommend any treatment that he didn't have confidence in, Tom flew with the patient to the clinic in California. Together they drank wheatgrass juice, ate sprouts, and ingested pureed watermelon fiber for a week. When they came home, Tom had lost ten pounds, and the patient's cancer went into remission for several years as he incorporated wheatgrass juice into his diet.

Another time, one of Tom's patients insisted he try a home remedy that was guaranteed to flush gallstones out of the gall bladder. Tom convinced me I should try the recipe with him. Together we drank Coke, lemon juice, and olive oil in proportions that promised to expedite the release of tiny green stones into the toilet with the next purging of the bladder. We moaned all night, fought nausea, and held our cramping stomachs. But staring into the toilet, hoping for a rewarding medical miracle, neither of us discovered the elusive gallstones. However, that is not to say the procedure doesn't work. Tom always insisted that every remedy will not work on every person in the same way. And he did have one patient bring him a jar full of tiny green stones gleaned from the toilet after performing this same "flush."

The magnets were different. They actually worked with a degree of consistency. Although there are many facets of alternative medicine that are not legitimate, Tom was delightfully surprised when a patient or a colleague recommended something that did work. Through another physician, he learned about the availability and application of Nikken magnets. Though not a cure-all, they definitely assisted in healing stubborn wounds and relieving some types of chronic pain. After he had sent a diabetic patient to the wound clinic for an open sore on her leg that stubbornly refused to heal after six months, he presented the option of trying a less conventional method of treatment. With her permission, he wrapped the magnet over the wound. Both Tom and the patient were amazed as healing occurred in a matter of weeks.

The objective was to be healed or get relief; the process that achieved that result was not as important to Tom as the result itself. He encouraged the use of a good vitamin and recommended some natural supplements for prostate care and blood-pressure maintenance. He also administered chelation therapy to patients who had researched the treatment and felt they would benefit from it. Many of the people, especially from the plain communities, who did not elect to have heart surgery when recommended, had shown marked improvements from chelation therapy.

Tom's biggest objection to alternative medicine was the claim by so many companies that their product would do things it did not do for everyone who tried it. Some products have some benefit, he would say; but many products had inconsistent results.

Regardless of the method, there was no greater joy for Tom than watching patients recover or finding ways to alleviate their suffering, especially if he could do it without deflating the patients' pocket-book. He always looked for ways to cut patients' costs, sometimes at his own expense. Because of his tendency to cut himself a little short financially, the office girls had to keep an eye on the income. They would often reprimand him for not charging a fee or for charging too little. Tom would cut other "superfluous" expenses to make sure he didn't have to charge too much for the necessary ones. One year, that backfired on him.

Tom refused to pay his dues for membership in the Indiana Academy of Family Physicians. The fee for members had increased incrementally over the years, and Tom decided it was time to stop paying the exorbitant annual dues. During one of these years, he was nominated for the Family Physician of the Year Award. Since he was not eligible for the award without membership, he did not receive the honor; however, he did receive a copy of the letter that recommended him:

> We would like to nominate for the Family Physician of the Year Award the name of Thomas R. Anderson, MD, whose office is located in Camden, Indiana.
>
> His practice could be characterized as outstanding. After many years of dealing with doctors within a good portion of the state of Indiana, many on a personal basis, we feel this man is deserving of the award. He towers over most of his fellow physicians in terms of compassionate care and success in providing needed healthcare for his patients.
>
> Truly a trusted friend of the people in his serving circles, he is sincerely interested in and personally devoted to the good health of his patients and their families. His desire to adequately and successfully

fulfill his calling as a family healthcare provider is evident in his watchful attention to all aspects of his clients' healthcare requirements and treatment.

His approach to practicing medicine has led to a tremendous increase in the number of families seeking his services. His practice now reaches families from several surrounding counties which include not just Carroll County, but also Tippecanoe, White, Howard, Clinton, and others as well. Patients think nothing of driving many miles just to secure his helpful services and treatment.

In order to serve those who are not financially able to afford many healthcare services, he built an addition on his home, housing several examination rooms, where he is available personally to care for such individuals, as well as to handle emergencies and other health maintenance performances. Such concern and dedication to the welfare of many families could be considered indicative of the highest caliber of professional service.

He makes house calls on individuals needing care who are unable to travel to his office. Several of these cases lately have been terminal cases. This excellent aspect of his practice is unheard of in many areas.

We personally feel this public servant, a family man himself, a role-model for many young people, a community leader, and a down-to-earth person who is always friendly, cordial, approachable, and helpful where he may be, merits the highest consideration for the Family Physician of the Year Award.

As he is held in the highest regard by residents of this area of Indiana, we would appreciate your taking into account these above mentioned unusual and extraordinary features when considering this nomination.

Tom kept the letter in his files. It meant a great deal to him to be nominated. However, I don't believe he ever paid his dues again for membership in the academy.

The office experience was full of memorable, rewarding moments that stirred a wide range of emotions. I remember the day a concerned patient had given her urine specimen in the bathroom cup, not realizing that she had grabbed the cup full of potpourri instead of an empty cup. She thought she had a serious disease when she saw brown leaflets and dried flowers floating in her pee.

Or there was the day Linda thought someone had gotten terribly sick in the toilet. She flushed and flushed, but the large obstacle would not go down. Being humble, gracious, and absolutely devoted to the welfare of the practice, she decided to clean the toilet out with her hands. After all, it was the toilet the patients used; it couldn't be blocked! Linda pulled the strangest looking obstruction from the water and showed it to Dr. Anderson with grave concern, thinking that one of the patients had an alarming problem.

"That's my lunch!" Tom gasped between non-stop hysterics. "It's chicken. It tasted disgusting, so I threw it in the toilet!"

Tom was often teasing either the staff or the patients. One day, one of the office helpers was preparing a woman for a pelvic exam. Tom decided he would not mention that the woman had an artificial leg. When the helper attempted to guide the patient's leg into the stirrup at the foot of the bed, the leg slid off into her hands. Tom just roared. He said he had never seen such a look on someone's face.

On one occasion, the laugh was on Tom. A desperate patient had come with a bowel impaction. Tom could have sent him to the emergency room, but he knew the cost and discomfort that would be involved. He cleaned out the bowel impaction, which exploded all over him. After calling home for a change of clothes and washing everything thoroughly, Tom continued to smell feces. Finally, he realized there were feces stuck in his bushy beard. From then on, the women in the office reminded him to check his beard.

There were, of course, the sad times too, such as when a young husband was diagnosed with cancer, when a little girl developed a brain tumor, and when he had to tell a spouse that their loved one had Alzheimer's disease. Many times, Tom sat gloomily at night and grieved over the patients whose suffering he could not relieve. Thankfully, the love and support of his patients helped him through such times.

Alzheimer's disease ravaged so many couples. It lightened his load just a little when one of his elderly patients, who wrote back and forth to his "older" sister, sent him the following letter:

I Can't Remember Poem

Just a line to say I'm living, that I'm not among the dead.
Though I'm getting more forgetful and mixed up in the head.
I got used to my arthritis, to my dentures I'm resigned.
I can manage my bifocals, but, God, I miss my mind.
For sometimes I can't remember when I stand at the foot of the stair,
If I must go up for something, or have I just come down from there?
And before the fridge so often, my mind is filled with doubt,
Have I just put food away or have I come to take some out?

And there are times when it is dark, with my nightcap
on my head,
I don't know if I'm retiring or just getting out of bed.
So, if it's my turn to write you, there's no need for
getting sore,
I may think that I have written and don't want to be
a bore.
So, remember that I love you and wish that you were
near.
But, now it's nearly mail time, so I must say "Good-
bye, Dear."
P.S. Here I stand beside the mailbox with a face so
very red,
Instead of mailing you my letter, I have opened it
instead.

For the most part, the Camden office was an atmosphere of
friendliness, comfort, and laughter. Three of our four children
eventually became part-time staff, working their way up from
emptying the trash to becoming a receptionist or medical assistant.
Although the youngest didn't become an employee, she spent
many hours reading books in the waiting room and drawing
pictures at Daddy's desk. For all of us, family, staff, and patients,
it was a place of community and caring.

CHAPTER 13

PATIENTS UNDERGROUND

THERE WERE THE REGULAR PATIENTS, and then there were the underground patients. I called them the underground patients because they were a secretive bunch for the most part. Like members of an underground church, they came furtively, glancing over their shoulder to see who shadowed them with reproach. If they came to the office, they often didn't want to explain their reasons for coming. Sometimes they didn't know how to explain; they just knew that something was wrong.

Several times, these types of patients came quietly to our home, or Tom and I visited with them in their home. They were the ones who suffered from mental and emotional illnesses such as depression or manic-depressive disorder. These were often Christians who came bearing the shame of an illness that neither they nor their church fellowship understood. Condemnation for being treated medically often plagued these people. Lack of understanding and information often hindered them from asking for help until they were painfully impaired by their illness. They were frightened.

One such woman waited patiently in our living room as Tom spoke with her. She sat quietly in the leather, wingback chair, hands clenched in her lap, head bowed, her eyes staring at the polished wood floor beneath her feet. She was gaunt from weight loss and glassy-eyed from sleepless nights.

Tom asked her, "Have you been feeling pretty sad lately, crying a lot?"

"Yes. I am so miserable, I just about wish I were dead," she answered, barely lifting her eyes to meet his.

Tom scooted his rocking chair close to her and urged gently, "Will you tell me what's going on in your life?"

"Well," she stated, flatly, "I guess I've had a lot of stress. Our son has been hospitalized again. I worry about him. I've been extremely busy at the pre-school where I teach. My husband is having a hard time handling our son's bouts of sickness. I don't think he knows how to express his fears and concerns. And I buried my mom last winter. We were pretty close. I don't think any of these things are unmanageable; it's just that I seem overwhelmed by everything right now. I'm not sleeping and not eating much. I seem to be really anxious all the time. I'm overwhelmed just trying to keep up with daily responsibilities."

"Listen," Tom explained, "sounds like you're dealing with some depression. Sometimes it affects people who are dealing with a lot of stress or grief, and other times it seems to strike without reason. But it's very treatable."

"I've heard and read about depression, but I've never experienced it. This is horrible," she moaned, covering her face with her hands. "I told my sister that I thought I might be depressed. She's convinced I am experiencing a demonic attack. She brought her pastor to the house to pray for me. He told me I didn't need anything but prayer and instruction in spiritual warfare."

Tom leaned back in his chair, clasped his hands together, and rested them behind his head before he spoke. "You bring that pastor to me when he has chest pain; we'll see if he wants prayer or nitroglycerin. You know, when I was a student at the University of Iowa Medical School, we always had a crowded emergency room during and after a football game. Emotions ran high. Next thing you know, fellows that just ate six hot dogs and downed several beers were in the ER with symptoms of a heart attack. People showed up all the time with chest pain during a game. How do you explain that? You see, what we experience in our emotions can have repercussions in our physical body. It happens all the time. People get stressed, and we have to treat them for high blood pressure. I don't know why people have such a hard time realizing that stress can cause a negative response in our emotional well-being as much as in our physical well-being. Why is treating one part of our body acceptable while treating another part is not? It's true that we understand a heart attack or a broken leg, whereas we can't see depression in the physical realm. But, believe me, depression is just as real, just as painful, and usually takes longer to heal."

"But, I know how some people at my church feel about medicating for emotional illnesses," the woman said. They think taking a pill for feeling depressed is kind of like taking an amphetamine off the street."Tom put his hands on the arm of the rocking chair, leaned back, and laughed, "Don't my patients wish they could get high from antidepressants! Anybody that tells you antidepressant medication for serious depression makes you high is just ignorant. Antidepressants can't and don't make clinically depressed people experience a happy high. They work slowly to increase the number of neurotransmitters in the brain, which, in turn, can help alleviate the state of depression. A patient will eventually return to normal functioning. That's about as exciting as it gets. Besides, if you could really get high on antidepressants, they would have some street value. Believe me, there are no drug cartels smuggling Zoloft. There's no buzz for the buck."

Gradually, the woman's fears were resolved enough for her to accept a prescription for antidepressants. As she walked out the door and drove slowly down the driveway, I turned to Tom and asked, "Do you think she'll fill the prescription?"

"Yes, she's an intelligent woman. She'll go home and do some research about depression and the medication used to treat it. Then she'll fill the prescription and get better. But she probably won't tell her sister or her church fellowship."

The woman was typical of many patients who were afraid to accept treatment for what has been termed a "mental illness." Tom always felt that, even with all of our medical advancements, the disorders that affect the brain remain the most complex and challenging. Particularly among religious communities, he found an aversion and a stigma associated with accepting medication for such maladies. It was very sad to watch people endure months or years of suffering when medication could often restore them to normal functioning.

Both men and women came who were combating symptoms of depression ranging anywhere from insomnia and loss of appetite to anger, anxiety, and suicidal thoughts. As people grew older, it was very common for them to experience an episode of depression. Tom often wondered why patients could understand the deterioration of the physical body in the aging process but failed to grasp the decline of the biological and chemical components affecting the brain.

"These bodies just weren't made to run forever," he would say.

Because of Tom's own experience with both depression and manic-depressive disorder, he could offer a great deal of compassion and understanding to his patients. Depression was fairly easy to diagnose and understand; manic-depressive disorder was a great deal more complicated. During an episode of mania, a patient could experience a euphoric phase that involved socially inappropriate behavior. This behavior could involve incessant talking, extremely poor judgment with financial decisions or with sexual encounters, hyper-activity with the inability to sleep, and sometimes a burst of creative energy that many people hate to lose when treated.

For a Christian, the devastation caused by an episode of manic behavior could leave them embarrassed and ashamed. The following period of depression was often greater due to guilt and regret. During one of Tom's episodes, he decided to repeat all the dirty jokes he had ever heard to every person he met. This was uncharacteristic behavior for him. He told the pharmacist, the neighbors, his patients, and our friends the most distasteful jokes ever heard. Later he put a pillow over his head and said, "Don't even tell me about it. I don't want to hear what I said. Just go away and leave me alone."

One of the worst symptoms of a manic episode is the lack of need for sleep. While Tom often thought putting an antidepressant in the local water supply would benefit at least half his patient population, treating the patients with manic-depressive symptoms was a lot more difficult. Sleep deprivation was a constant challenge. In frustration, patients would turn to alcohol or sleeping pills. Both of these substances would provide temporary relief but would soon require an increase in quantity to be effective. By the time some patients had the courage to see a physician; they needed help from Alcoholics Anonymous, which Tom encouraged them to join.

Financial disagreements between spouses also brought struggling patients to seek help. One couple sat quietly in the patient room. Tom knew the husband was a successful local businessman with manic-depressive disorder. He had treated him many times before. As he sat down on the gray leather stool and scooted close to the couple, he teasingly asked the wife, "So, what's he buying this week?"

"Well," she cringed slightly, "he bought a racehorse."

"It's a really good horse. I know it is," her husband interrupted. "I've read about them. Winning horses can bring in a lot of money. I think I might learn to ride myself. Horses love me. I'm really good with animals. This will be a good investment. I don't do anything and the horse makes money. Maybe I'll run this one in the Derby …"

Tom asked, "Have you ever had a horse before?"

"No," he said, "but I can learn how to manage one. People make a lot of money with racehorses."

"You got a jockey and a trainer and a place to keep it?" Tom asked.

"Oh, I'll find somebody to train him. Maybe I'll learn to ride him myself. I always wanted to do that. You know, if I had two horses, I would increase my chances of winning. Do you want to buy one with me? We could be partners. We sit in our offices while our horses make money for us. C'mon Doc, this could be our big win. Maybe we could buy a farm in Kentucky and raise a whole bunch of race-horses. I know we could do this. Look, I've got a list of good ones for sale," he said, pulling a folded paper from his pocket.

Tom put his hand on the man's arm. "Listen, we're going to need to adjust your medicine."

"You know," declared the patient, "I'm feeling really good. I don't think I need anything right now. Sometimes I get a little down, but I'm feeling great. I've got plans; things are going pretty well for me, and I'm recognizing opportunities that are going to pay off in the future. As a matter of fact, I bought a sailboat for my wife last week …"

Tom glanced at the wife, who nodded in agreement. "I see," he said. "We might need to do a little intervention."

With compassion and understanding, Tom treated the literal ups and downs of many patients who struggled with their disorder and with taking medication. He counseled the couple that came to him after the wife had crawled in bed with the refrigerator repair-man one afternoon during a manic episode. He explained to the shame-faced wife and the angry husband that not staying on the right medication could cause terrible lapses in judgment, particularly sexual or financial. I believe he saved a marriage that day.

When manic, Tom, like anyone with the disorder, loved to spend money, often impulsively. He ordered stainless-steel warming dishes along with all the accessories to entertain and feed large groups of people. He bought a horse and all the equipment to go with it. One time, he bought a motorcycle over his lunch hour. When not manic, Tom fretted incessantly over finances. As depression followed mania, financial concerns reached the point of an irrational fear, which is typical for depressed people.

Under normal circumstances, Tom was very frugal. In spite of his illness, he managed to purchase a small farm near our home and another, larger farm about a mile away, plus the house and acreage where we lived. For several years, I grew increasingly concerned about the way he spent money - frugal and wise at times, then impulsive and excessive at other times. But God intervened. He said, "Look, I own the cattle on a thousand hills. The earth is mine. The heavens are mine. It's just money. You need to love, honor, and respect your husband; I'll take care of the money." "It's just money" was a phrase that came back to me many times. It wasn't a phrase that I felt was very socially acceptable or politically correct in the United States of America, and sadly, probably not even in the church communities. But, in God's kingdom, I could see that He values things a little differently than we do here.

Yes, we should be wise and good stewards, but sometimes there are extenuating circumstances. Having a mental disorder that clouds your judgment is not a fair assessment of how a person handles money. Overall, Tom did an amazing job of providing and caring for his family in spite of the burdens he carried. He and I often laughed and said that being manic depressive is the sinner's dream disease. It allows its victims to say that they are sexually indiscreet, financially irresponsible, judgmentally impaired, and socially inappropriate because of an illness. Of course, on medication, the individual is less likely to exhibit such symptoms.

Because of what Tom endured, he was able to diagnose and treat people with much wisdom and compassion. Nevertheless, some patients continued to be very reluctant to seek treatment or medication for mental and emotional illnesses, either because of their misunderstanding and lack of knowledge, or because of their church fellowship. Some Christian communities discouraged their members from trying to alleviate, through medication, the experience of despondency, not understanding that the despondency of clinical depression or manic-depressive disorder is not normal and could be fatal if left untreated.

Of course, nobody ever worries much about people that are too happy or too energetic. And manic people can be very interesting. Talking to a person experiencing a manic episode can be especially entertaining. Tom's mind would race light-years ahead of the conversation then circle back with an outburst that was usually irrelevant to the present topic. He had picked up the gist of the conversation after word three. So, in his mind, he had been to Jupiter and back while waiting on the person to catch up with him. Everybody moved, talked, and lived in slow motion compared to his speed.

While manic people can get a lot accomplished, nobody really wants a mental disorder. Tom understood only too well the struggle his patients had with both the diagnoses and the treatment of mental and emotional illnesses. He and I often talked about the silent suffering of those who struggled with depression. The loneliness, isolation, and hopelessness of depression reminded us of a pastor's experience who had been held in isolation for three years. Forgotten, feeling alone, isolated from the world, and in the deep mental and emotional pain of torture and injustice, he suffered profoundly. Patients locked in the invisible cell of severe depression often experience some of the same responses, except no one sees their pain or understands their torment.

For these patients, Tom did what he could to comfort, educate, and provide medication. Through the years of his practice, he saw an increasing number of patients experiencing both depression and manic-depressive disorder. He forewarned that these mental illnesses would increase as our society becomes increasingly negligent in caring for and protecting their offspring. Although no one understands entirely, some research indicates that mental and emotional illnesses often follow childhood trauma, particularly abuse. Sometimes it is just a matter of a genetic predisposition. Nevertheless, it is an ever-increasing affliction.

Tom's own illness was growing worse with age. Periods of mania surfaced more regularly and to a greater extreme. As summer lazily rolled over into the autumn of 2008, Tom had an insatiable desire to build his long-awaited cabin. It was very poor timing in my estimation. We were in debt; money was tight. The expense of building a cabin seemed ridiculous. Once again, the Lord intervened. He touched my heart with the understanding that this was a dream Tom had carried since he was a young boy. I sold a truckload of lambs and as I handed Tom the check, I said, "I want you to have that cabin. You've waited a long time. Build it."

He did. Side by side, we stained the boards for the interior. With our daughter and son-in-law, we laid the deck. By Thanksgiving, most of the cabin was finished. It sits perched on the hillside beside the creek. It was the last project we did together.

Tom was the caring, understanding physician for many people with mental and emotional illnesses. And I cared for Tom. As the years passed, I learned that the only genuine, enduring love comes from God. "Let me see with your eyes; let me love with your love" became my prayer. As the years passed, I saw Tom's personal pain and struggle with his own illness as well as the individual he was beneath the complex disorder. Tom Anderson was simply the finest man I have ever known.

CHAPTER 14

THANKSGIVING 2008

It was nearing the Thanksgiving holiday. Our oldest daughter, now a high-school English teacher, had married a Purdue graduate who was part of the Lafayette police force. They lived in West Lafayette, but would be home for Thanksgiving dinner. Our oldest son, with his wife, lived in Pennsylvania, where he attended medical school. They didn't plan on coming for Thanksgiving because of the drive and the short vacation. Our youngest son decided to visit his brother in Pennsylvania for the holidays. That left our thirteen-year-old baby girl at home.

But our Thanksgiving dinner table would not be empty. We were looking forward to our nephew, his wife, and their children, who traditionally spent Thanksgiving with us. They had arrived, and the house was taking on that holiday feel. Children were laughing, pots and pans were banging, and fires crackled in the woodstoves. Tom loved to make the day special with a new dish or a different bread recipe. The smell of garlic croutons wafted through the house on many holidays when Tom prepared his Caesar salad. This evening, he was busy marinating the turkey while children were getting ready for bed and the game board was being set up for the adults to play Settlers of Catan. Tom never played board games, saying they were "bored" games.

As wives often do, I sensed Tom's heart was troubled. When he disappeared to the basement, I followed him. Sitting on the floor outside his bathroom door, I waited for him. He opened the door and slid down beside me on the cold cement.

"What's wrong?" I asked.

"I'm failing," he said.

"What do you mean?" I asked.

"I'm not the man I want to be. I can't keep everything together. Maybe tomorrow, maybe tomorrow I can try again. Maybe I will do better tomorrow." He sighed.

Once again, I could see the depression wrapping itself around him, the stress of the manic-depressive disorder overcoming him, and the haunting tragedy of his childhood experience pilfering away at his emotional stability like a fast-growing cancer.

"Tom, listen. I will do more to help you."

"Will you? Will you help me?" he pleaded.

I touched his cheek. "You know I will. Tomorrow we will try harder to beat this thing. We will figure out something together."

I stood up and took his hand. After pulling him to his feet, I walked slowly up the basement stairs. He followed me. As I sat down to the board game, he reached out and gently squeezed my shoulder. Tomorrow we would solve the problems.

But could I put the pieces back together from his broken childhood? Could I stop the onslaught of the mental disorder that was worsening each year? Could I put an end to the excruciating pain from his deepening depressions and the isolation that haunted him no matter how many people surrounded him? I knew that I could not do these things. I did not know about tomorrow.

We played games and laughed and went to bed, anticipating our family dinner and fun the following day. At about 4:30am, Tom got up to go to the bathroom and fell to the floor.

"Tom, what's the matter?" I asked, alarmed.

"I can't get up. Just throw me a pillow and let me stay right here," he said sleepily.

"No, you can't stay on the floor. You'll get cold. Let me help you." I tried to lift him to the bed.

"No, my back hurts. Don't do anything. Just let me rest."

With three back surgeries over the years and his recent complaints of back pain, I did not want to cause more injury or discomfort. Stretching across the bed to the phone on the bedside table, I called our son in medical school. While I discussed Tom's symptoms, his snoring resumed. He was notorious for his loud, rocks-sliding-down-the-mountain snoring, so I thought he had fallen back to sleep … until the snoring stopped. Then there is that moment when silence screams.

I hung up the phone and frantically called the ambulance. Pounding on my nephew's door, I got help to perform CPR. The lights were on, footsteps were running, a path was being cleared for the stretcher. But somewhere in the deep recesses of my mind, I knew that Tom was gone.

My daughter and I trailed the ambulance to the nearest town in my husband's car. Driving his car, I sensed his presence. His Tic Tac mints were on the seat, along with a pair of gray, wool gloves. His music CD was on the floor.

We walked into the hospital emergency room. How many hospitals had I entered to find him, to take him lunch, to bring his children to visit to him? The same smells, the same highly polished floors, white lab coats, push carts of glass tubes, and swinging doors. Someone ushered us to a side room, where the doctor said that he was sorry. It was probably an aneurism followed by a heart attack.

How surreal it is to stand with your daughter and stare at the bloated, blue-tinged body of your husband. Yes, it was his body. No, it wasn't him. His laughter, his kindness, his remarkable diagnostic skills, his warm and competent hands, his quick and brilliant mind were not there in that body or that room.

I drove the car home from the hospital with my daughter to a house full of family but a house so empty. Before nine o'clock that morning, I received calls from Tennessee, California, and Pennsylvania, asking if it was true that Dr. Tom was gone. Yes, friends, he is gone.

There are things that a person must do when a loved one dies. People have to be called, a funeral must be planned, and decisions have to be made. For once, we did not have a casket in our attic, but Herman brought us a simple, walnut-stained poplar casket made by the Amish man. The children came home, and we did the things that needed to be done, helping each other.

Both the funeral director and the pastor of the church where we held the funeral were patients of Tom's. They were especially kind and helpful. Tom's family came. And then the funeral came. Through tears, I saw the friends of a lifetime stand speechless, weeping, beside the casket of a man who had cried with them, laughed with them, and cared deeply for them.

Each member of our immediate family spoke briefly at the funeral, but our oldest son said so well what was on our hearts.

> My father was a great man. If you knew my father at all, then you know what a great loss each and every one of us here today has suffered. He was my mentor, my hero, and my friend. He taught me that anything is possible, and he enabled me to make all my goals and dreams become reality. But, most of all, he taught me to have compassion.

He poured his heart and soul into caring for people. He loved people no matter what. It didn't matter if you were rich or poor, young or old. It didn't matter which church you went to or what your politics were, he loved you just for being you.

I am currently in medical school. So many of my classmates talk about how they want to go into some lucrative specialty where they can work in a big hospital in a big city, make a bunch of money, and be a big shot, because that is what they believe will make them a success. Dad was a brilliant man, and if he had wanted to do that, he could have. But he chose to practice here, in Carroll County, because he loved this community.

There are children here who were born in his house. There are many of you here who became ill and were taken into his home to be cared for. Some of you, I know, are alive today because of him. Each and every one of you today is here because Tom Anderson impacted your life in some way.

My father left this life to be with God on Thanksgiving morning, but the influence of his life did not and should not end there. Let his memory live on in all of you. If you want to honor my father and his life and what it meant, then when you think of him, tell your family that you love them, tell your friends that you are there for them. Seek out the people in this community who are in need and help them. That's what his life was all about. He is gone now, but he will live on in all of us in a small way when we take the time to love each other.

A friend, former patient, and pastor's wife sang Tom's favorite hymn: "It Is Well With My Soul." After singing with her beautiful voice, she said, "A great physician has met the great Physician."

We buried him in our family cemetery just up the road from our home. The man who sold headstones was also a patient of Tom's. He knew the stone Tom wanted, and he gave it as a gift. It was a black granite bench. Tom always said folks ought to be able to sit down in the cemetery; even in death, he thought of the needs of others. We had the words *Beloved Physician, Husband, Father, and Friend* carved into the stone.

For almost twenty years, we had been members and active participants in the home-schooling community. A dear friend, neighbor, and home-schooling mother wrote a tribute in Tom's honor.

> Unforgettable. A phone call came on Thursday morning, Thanksgiving Day, sharing the news of the passing of Dr. Tom Anderson. Friday, a busy but hushed kitchen at the Anderson home hosts people coming with food and leaving with whispered words difficult to say and to hear. On Saturday, a large sanctuary shelters a clustered gathering of family at the head, strong and solid; mementos and tributes to husband, father, son arranged carefully and lovingly among bursts of colorful flowers. People who loved Tom Anderson and his family wait, then hesitantly move toward the front to mingle, embrace, encourage, and grieve.

> Unforgettable. It is the same sanctuary with seams stretching as mourners crowd to give respect to a unique man. His wife enters and with a quiet calm leads their children to a place where none of them wants to be.

Unforgettable. The pastor shares glimpses of a man ministering in his church, a man intricately woven into the fabric of his community; a man whose medical practice was more than a prescription or a way to make a living, but an extension of the man himself, a humble, strong, kind doctor. He was a doctor who made deliberate, daily choices to be available to the sick. Jointly, and with one great sigh, we remember.

Unforgettable. Tom's wife, two daughters, and two sons stir our hearts with tender memories; lift our eyes with promises of the future; inspire our spirits with their tribute to the pivotal influence this man had in the direction of their lives; and empower our helplessness with a challenge to fill the void left by a compassionate man.

Unforgettable. Dr. Tom Anderson is unforgettable. His love for his family, his humble service and hospitality to his fellow man, and his commitment to God has long-reaching arms that will affect generations.

We at Follow the Light of Christ Co-op will sorely miss Dr. Anderson. He has impacted many of our families with his hospitality and with the classes he taught. Pictures of Dr. Anderson making Caesar salad at a formal dinner, dancing the Funky Chicken in his living room, or supervising the dissection of an organ will be causes for future smiles as we remember. While we may question, God's timing is certain and perfect. Tom Anderson just beat us home!

Yes, Tom had gone home. But there was such a void that he left behind! So many people were devastated by the loss of their physician and friend. Cards and letters filled the mailbox.

CHAPTER 15

LETTERS

A^FTER A FUNERAL, PEOPLE GO home. The family and the spouse attempt to find a routine that doesn't exist. Only those who have walked through such a valley of sorrow can know even a shadow of the pain. My heart was touched by the number of letters that came to comfort, to remember, and to encourage. Some people sent money. Our dear friend Howard, from Canada, sent a generous check, saying that he didn't want me to worry about the next mortgage payment. His kindness and thoughtfulness touched my heart. Some of the letters I have kept as treasures. A fellow physician sent a short note that spoke volumes,

"I was deeply saddened to hear about Tom. He was one of my heroes. He acted as a physician and as a person like, ideally, how I think God wants us to act. He was the gold standard. He shared God's love (with your support and help) with so many thousands of people, and all of us will miss him."

Many letters came, some with memories to share, some with inconsolable grief. One of Tom's patients wrote a letter to the newspaper. It was published the week his office was closed permanently by the company he had associated himself with.

Dr. Thomas R. Anderson, his wonderful staff, and his office in Camden provided a secure and safe haven for his patients. The office was decorated with a touch of Early-American and country-style décor.

His office not only portrayed that era of American history, but Dr. Anderson himself offered the special care of those doctors in that time of our American heritage. He reminds us of the caring doctor of yesteryear. In our country, in the present day, he was a one-of-a-kind physician.

… People of the community loved their doctor. Many traveled long distances to see him. … He traveled the extra mile for his patients. He went above and beyond. He had an uncanny ability not only to understand a person's health but also to understand a person's personality, heart, mind, and soul. He listened with compassion and empathy, and gave encouragement and hope. His deep beliefs, values, and generosity inspired and influenced many.

It is with deep grief to think of an empty office with the echoes of all the past joy, warmth, wisdom, and care of Dr. Anderson and his staff. … The community has suffered a great and profound loss.

We are grieving in spirit with Dr. Anderson's family, staff, and many other patients. It will be difficult to continue without him and his staff. …

In deepest gratitude and sympathy we thank his loving family and his caring staff. It is a great honor and privilege to have known such an extraordinary doctor.

I was grateful that people took time to share their appreciation, their grief, and their sense of loss, because we, as Tom's family, acutely felt the same irreplaceable absence. But we grieved for the loss of husband and father. The letter that tugged my heartstrings the most was a journal entry written the following year by our then fourteen-year-old daughter.

> The pain is a bruise. Sometimes it spreads to my hands and makes them tremble. Other times it touches my feet and makes me stumble. The worst times, it spreads to my face when I think no one is looking, and it makes me crumble. At all times, though, it stays at my heart. A sickening shade of black, it throbs, always throbs. It is not totally content to just throb, though. One touch over that tender spot, and a pain so sharp, so painful, so pitiful, seers through me till I am on my knees, sobbing for relief.

> It hurts on my birthday when I realize he is not here and never will be again. It hurts when I look in the mirror and see the blue eyes he gave me staring back. It hurts when I want to hug him, and he isn't here. Most of all, it hurts to know that in the thirteen years we had, I did not really know him at all. We would have gotten along well, I am told. We are so alike, they say. I hate it. I hate being reminded of what could have been. I hate knowing that there was someone just like me, but now they are gone.

> The bruise is throbbing again. The sharp pain has passed, and I am left with nothing, but a dull ache and a catch in my throat. Tears dry, leaving salty trails down my face. They itch. I take a shaky breath, and somehow, I feel better. I do not know why. By all accounts, I should still be sobbing. I will still cry;

I will still hurt; I will still bruise. But I will live. My
dad is gone, but I am still here and I will go on.

Like everyone else, we remembered, grieved, struggled,
shared our pain, and slowly found ways to take steps in a forward
direction.

CHAPTER 16

WHEN BIRDS FLY

I OFTEN CROSS PATHS WITH PEOPLE who were Tom's patients. Sometimes they will tell me they have been to the cemetery to sit on the bench and talk to Doc. It helps, they say. I, too, visit the cemetery. Brushing my hand over the words carved into the granite bench, I speak as if Tom were just on the other side of a veil. "Martha and Daniel live in the house now. They have a baby boy who toddles up and down the hallways. He reminds me of your baby pictures. You would have loved taking him to the office with you. Of course, you would have told everyone he was the smartest little boy in the county – just like his grandpa. Ben graduated from medical school. I wish you could have been there to share that moment. You would have been so proud. He was second in his class, just like you. Ben and Amanda are going to have a baby in December. We're so excited for them. Sam is at Purdue now, studying pre-med and in love with Laura. You would like her a lot. Lily is so much like you. She loves to tan hides and study the sciences. You would have had so much fun with her. Of course, you would have spoiled her."

Sitting on the bench, I watch the leaves catch in the wind and a sparrow land to scratch the dirt. Processing thirty years of marriage to a remarkable person takes time. Tom's mother once said that, while most of us walk through life holding a candle, Tom ran with a blow torch. I have to smile at that all-too-true image. In his short lifespan of fifty-four years, he did so much.

I learned lessons from my husband that I hope I will never forget. He taught me the value of cherishing and protecting our children; he taught me about following Jesus; and he taught me to live even when life is hard.

Because of Tom, I know that children are truly a gift from God. They are beautiful, fragile, and so easily damaged or molded for greatness. They desperately need our nurturing care and protection. A happy childhood is an irreplaceable, immeasurably valuable gift we can give our children, but it takes time and sacrifice. It isn't about toys, opportunities, and things; it's about being together, being loved, and knowing that you are worth the time and attention it takes to say, "You are the most important person on the planet to me, and I will sacrifice my life for you."

When Matthew 18:6 says, "But whoso shall offend one of these little ones which believe in me, it were better for him that a millstone were hanged about his neck, and that he were drowned in the depth of the sea," I understand something of God's heart for the children. A day of reckoning will come. For individuals and for nations that neglect and defile the innocent, there will be great judgment.

In the meantime, those children grow up and struggle with the repercussions of evil perpetrated against them. Especially for the little boys subjected to sexual violation, there is a wound so deep and profound that few have been able to find help or healing. Instead, they suffer in silence and shame.

As Christians, we tell these shattered vessels that they are "new creations in Christ" and that freedom and change awaits them in the Christian walk. But the truth is that the victims carry very deep wounds and heavy burdens every day of their life. They stumble some days and overcome some days, but they battle the repercussions of abuse to their graves. The miracle is that these brothers and sisters live and function at all.

As a Christian community and even a secular community, we have failed grievously in our ability to minister to or counsel adult victims of childhood sexual abuse and molestation. Their wounds scar every part of their humanity: emotions, mind, and physical well-being, as well as their spiritual health. By walking beside Tom, I got a tiny glimpse of the isolation, the shame, the longing to start over in life without all the baggage, and the terrible fear of being so messed up that you might hurt someone you love.

In spite of the scars Tom carried, I saw God use him to give care and compassion to others. Out of his brokenness, God's glory was able to flow unhindered by the confidence and strength so many "normal" individuals possess. And every day for thirty years, I sensed God's tremendous love and care for Tom. Our heavenly Father knows, sees, and understands the most broken and confused human heart.

Tom taught me about Jesus. He was nineteen when he committed his life to Christ. There wasn't much religion in Tom's life, just Jesus. For him, following Jesus meant reading the Bible and doing what it said. When it said to take care of the man on the side of the road, Tom did. He never asked about that man's religion, education, moral standards, financial state, or social standing. He never insisted that the man eventually get up and join him in his side-of-the road ministry. He just picked the man up and carried him to a better place - because that's what Jesus told us to do.

The gospel, as Tom understood it, was in Matthew 25:35: "For I was hungry and you gave Me food; I was thirsty and you gave Me drink; I was a stranger, and you took Me in; I was naked and you clothed me; I was sick and you visited Me; I was in prison and you came to Me." This is the gospel that Tom understood and practiced.

Periodically, Tom would take a job at the state mental hospital, which was in a near-by town. He deeply loved these patients who were often irreparably damaged victims of childhood sexual abuse. A couple of times, he had the hospital staff bring the patients to our home to see the animals, have dessert, and ride the tractor. A lot of people wouldn't spend their time and efforts on such "lost" souls. But Tom loved them. He treated them like honored guests, because Jesus would.

Tom taught me to live in the midst of hardship. Because I watched him live with inner pain and turmoil for thirty years, I knew I couldn't give up, even though losing him brought overwhelming grief and sorrow. I continued to breathe, to take baby steps forward, and to struggle through the next day. Living life without being at Tom's side seemed impossible at first. Surely God made a mistake when He failed to call us home together. Why would He make us "one" through life, then call one of us home and leave the other behind? My sister-in-law had given me a plaque one Christmas with the framed words of Martin Buxbaum: "May there be such a oneness between you in your marriage that when one of you weeps, the other will taste salt." I had carried Tom's pain with him, and I tasted salt many times. Daily, I watched him walk down a very difficult road in spite of the demons that hounded him, in spite of incalculable silent suffering, in spite of battle fatigue that frayed the fabric of his soul. It takes courage to live with pain. Every day that Tom lived, he showed me courage.

I sit on the bench in the cemetery and watch the sparrow fly away. It lands lightly on a distant branch. But I have watched other birds, ones that tumble out of the nest too early. They are injured in the fall or damaged by an overzealous predator that has been waiting to pounce. For one reason or another, they are hindered in their flight. Abused children are like birds with broken wings; they can't fly far or high or for very long, if they fly at all. Tom was one of those wounded ones. But when he gave his life to

Christ, the wind currents swept him up and took him to heights that most of us will never reach.

Standing, my words are carried on a gentle breeze, "I miss you, Tom." His heart speaks to mine, "Take good care of the children." Leaving the cemetery, I drive the short distance home. In my closet is Tom's red-and-black plaid jacket. We replaced his worn-out one several years ago. I brush my hand down the rough wool of the sleeve. Reaching over to the dresser, I pull a bottle of his cologne close to my nose and sniff, squeezing back my tears. A line from one of Tom's favorite hymns by Lizzie DeArmond, hums its way into my memory "When we step from this earth to God's heaven so fair, we'll say 'good night' here but 'good morning' up there." I'll see you in the morning, Tom, my heart whispers. On that day, he will be whole, healthy, washed clean from the baggage he had to carry on earth. He will be as free as the eagles that soar among the mountaintops.